Make Your Website a Money Machine

A Guide to Marketing Funnels for Websites

by

Howie Todoit

Dear Esteemed Reader,

Thank you immensely for choosing this book to join your collection. We imagine that you've already embarked on an exploration of ideas within these pages, and we couldn't be happier about it!

Now, if you find yourself chuckling, pondering, or even debating with the words in front of you, we'd absolutely love to hear about it. If you can spare a few moments to pen down your thoughts in a review, we would be as delighted as a dictionary on a spelling bee!

An Amazon review would be excellent - but hey, we're far from picky. Whether it's a scribble on the back of a grocery list, a tweet, or even a message in a bottle (though that might take a while to reach us), your feedback is gold.

Writing a review might not be as fun as a spontaneous dance-off, but we promise it'll bring grins to our faces, warmth to our hearts, and incredibly valuable insights to future readers.

With Gratitude,

Bo Bennett, PhD
Publisher
Archieboy Holdings, LLC.

CONTENTS

CHAPTER 1: INTRODUCTION

Launching an online business comes with its unique set of challenges. From setting up a website that embodies your brand identity to driving relevant traffic and turning visitors into customers, it's a journey that requires dedication, strategy, and a willingness to learn. But what if there was an approach that could streamline this process, funneling potential customers from the point of discovery to the point of purchase seamlessly? This book aims precisely to guide you to create a marketing funnel that maximizes sales of your products or services.

If you think about the most successful businesses of this digital era, it isn't too hard to note they all share a common trait - a well-defined marketing funnel. This innovative approach empowers business owners to guide customers through the buying process strategically. Your website is not just an online storefront; in the hands of a savvy entrepreneur, it can become a powerful conveyor belt of conversion.

Before diving deep into those practical steps, it's essential to understand the unique opportunities at your fingertips. Today, an online business isn't confined to the limits of physical reach. It doesn't demand the overhead costs of brick-and-mortar operations nor does it require one to adhere to the conventional nine-to-five grind. It sets the stage for you to cross geographic boundaries, connect with discerning consumers, and literally have your business available round the clock.

Beneath the allure of such vast potential, it's crucial to remember that a successful online business leaves nothing to guesswork. Every step, from choosing your website's platform to planning your growth, is part of a well-orchestrated plan. Web traffic may arrive from countless sources, your marketing funnel ensures that you can guide them along the path to purchase, increasing the likelihood of conversion.

Creating your marketing funnel needn't be a daunting task. The aim here is to break down each step, providing a thorough understanding before we move to implementing each strategy. Whether you're a solopreneur or a manager leading a team, this book is designed to equip you with the knowledge to establish an effective marketing funnel for your online business.

So where do we begin? Remember, every journey begins with a single step. In this case, it's understanding the fundamentals of an online business. Once we've laid a good foundation, we'll explore the concept of a marketing funnel and how it works, delving into each stage, from awareness to advocacy. Knowledge is power, and understanding this process gives you the power to drive sales and encourage customer loyalty.

As we delve into the technical aspects of building your website, you'll find guidance on picking a platform that suits your business, as well as key elements that make a site both appealing to visitors and effective in driving conversions. We'll discuss web design, compelling content, and the importance of SEO in boosting your website's visibility in the digital realm.

Next, expect to take a deep dive into the creation of your marketing funnel. From defining your target market to strategies that attract the right audience, this module will lay out the tools and techniques necessary to draw potential customers into your funnel. We'll explore content creation, social media marketing, and email marketing as potential sources of lead generation.

We'll then transition into the implementation phase of your marketing funnel, providing practical guidance on landing pages, lead magnets, automatic emails, sales pages, and payment gateways. These techniques translate your marketing efforts into tangible sales.

But remember, it doesn't end there. We'll also cover how to optimize this funnel, analyze data, test variants, and optimize conversion rates. Your ability to refine and improve your marketing efforts is what will give you an edge over competitors.

This book also aims to help you expand your online presence through affiliate marketing, social networking, and paid advertising. These tactics can all work synergistically to lift your brand recognition and draw in more potential customers.

We understand that establishing an online business and setting up an effective marketing funnel comes with its challenges. Many obstacles may seem overwhelming. But don't worry, we've got you covered. Common struggles such as handling customer objections, addressing technical issues, and keeping up with market trends will be discussed so that you're equipped to tackle them head-on.

We'll wrap things up by presenting case studies of successful businesses that employ marketing funnels effectively. Understanding real-life examples will strengthen your comprehension of concepts and inspire you to apply these strategies creatively.

To conclude, the modern entrepreneur needs to master the art of the marketing funnel. This savvy approach takes potential customers on a controlled journey, from first contact to the point of purchase and beyond. This book will provide a roadmap to establishing such a funnel for your online business, empowering it to thrive in this dynamic digital age.

Chapter 2: The Basics of Online Business

As we delve into the foundational elements of online business, you'll soon realize why establishing a strong online presence is non-negotiable in today's digitally-driven market. Let's start with e-commerce, which is simply the buying and selling of goods or services using the internet. From multinational corporations to small businesses, e-commerce has become an indispensable aspect of modern commerce, an enabler of global trade, and a facilitator of efficient transactions. At the center of this is your website - your virtual storefront. It not only serves as a landing spot for your customers but crucially sets the stage for your marketing funnel, which we'll explore in more detail in subsequent chapters. Remember, a website is not just about aesthetics; it's the epicenter of your online business ecosystem where your product, value proposition, and customer interaction come together. So, understanding e-commerce and a website's significance in online marketing is quintessential in setting up an effective marketing funnel that will maximize your sales.

Understanding E-commerce

As you embark on your online business journey, the first step is understanding what e-commerce involves. E-commerce, also known as electronic commerce, primarily refers to selling products and services over the Internet. It transcends the traditional boundaries of a physical store, enabling businesses to reach customers from all corners of the globe.

E-commerce works in several ways, including B2C (business-to-consumer), B2B (business-to-business), C2C (consumer-to-consumer), and C2B (consumer-to-business).

Now, let's dive deeper into the fundamentals and structures of e-commerce so you can fully grasp its potential and learn to leverage it effectively.

B2C e-commerce is likely what you may think of first when discussing online business. It's the process of businesses selling directly to consumers. This model encompasses online retailers, service subscription sites, downloadable product vendors, and so on. It's most akin to the experience of shopping in a physical store, just transferred to an online setting.

B2B e-commerce, on the other hand, refers to trade between businesses. This can involve wholesalers selling to retailers, or manufacturers selling raw materials to a producer. In this model, volume is typically higher, with longer sales cycles, larger transactions, and greater buyer deliberation.

C2C e-commerce involves transactions between consumers, facilitated by a third-party platform. One classic example is eBay, where consumers can buy and sell from one another. This model gives business owners opportunities to observe trends and identify product interests on a micro level.

E-commerce also extends into the C2B model, where consumers can offer goods and services to companies. Freelance platforms are a primary example, where individuals can offer their skills, time, or products to businesses looking to outsource certain processes.

Regardless of the model, an e-commerce business involves significant planning and substantial attention to detail. Whether you're selling merchandise, downloadable content, or services, each facet of your business must be designed and executed with precision.

The core of every e-commerce business lies at its digital storefront— the website. Ensuring your site's accessibility, appeal, navigability, and simplicity are keys to your online business success. But we'll dive more into websites later. For now, let's concentrate on the mechanics of an e-commerce business— finding customers, making sales, and retaining those customers for life.

Finding customers in the expansive online world might seem daunting, but with the right targeting strategies, it's manageable and lucrative. You can reach your audience through organic search results or pay-per-click campaigns that direct individuals to your online store. We'll go more in-depth with customer acquisition strategies in the subsequent sections.

Then there's making sales online, which differs significantly from making sales in a physical location. That's where secure, user-friendly, and reliable payment systems come in, allowing straightforward transactions and instilling trust in your consumers. Further down this guide, we'll unravel the intricacies of online transactions.

Customer retention is crucial in e-commerce. Acquiring a new customer can cost up to five times more than retaining an existing customer. Hence, once you attract customers, it's essential to keep them coming back for more. Crucial customer retention strategies include providing excellent customer service, encouraging customer feedback, offering loyalty programs, and communicating regularly through engaging newsletters or email updates.

Moreover, it's critical to establish an efficient fulfillment approach that ensures quick, reliable delivery of physical goods. Given the speed with which consumers expect their online purchases delivered, having a smooth, efficient, and trustworthy supply chain process is a must.

Lastly, always remember that e-commerce is constantly evolving. It's an exciting, fast-paced world that offers massive opportunities for those willing to keep learning, adapting, and thriving. Regardless of how well you understand e-commerce, there's always room for innovation, optimization, and advancement. That's the dynamic nature of online business we all enthusiastically engage in.

Welcome to the world of e-commerce.

The Importance of a Website in Online Marketing

As we delve deeper into the world of online business, it becomes increasingly evident that having a website is integral to the success of your operations. It is more than just a digital calling card or a virtual storefront. A website serves as the hub of all your online marketing activities, the platform where all your efforts converge and culminate. It is the foundation stone on which the structure of your online business stands.

Your website is the online representation of your brand. Like a physical store, it gives your business a sense of identity and legitimacy. When customers need to know more about you, it's likely your website they'll visit first. It is your opportunity to make an unforgettable first impression. Leaving that impression to third-party platforms can be risky. Your website gives you full control over your brand message and image.

One of the biggest advantages of a website is its availability. Unlike a brick-and-mortar store, your website is open 24/7, available to anyone, anytime, anywhere. No matter what time zone your customers are in, they can access your products, services, and information at their convenience. When your website is your primary interaction point with your customers, time constraints are no longer an issue.

Another benefit of websites is the ability to reach a wider audience. Physical location is no barrier on the internet. With a website, your reach isn't limited to your local vicinity, city, or even your country. You can reach potential customers from all corners of the globe, expanding your market exponentially.

Your website also provides you with valuable data. With tools like Google Analytics, you can collect and analyze data from your website to understand your customers better. You can see where your visitors are coming from, what they're looking at on your site, and how long they're staying.

This information is crucial in formulating effective marketing strategies.

Furthermore, websites offer unparalleled opportunities for customer engagement. It's a platform where you can interact with your customers, take their feedback, resolve their issues, and even foster a community. They are also places where customers can leave reviews, testimonials, or comments. This interaction not only helps build relationships with your customers but also provides crucial social proof for your brand.

A well-designed website also serves as a cornerstone for your online marketing campaigns. It is the ultimate conversion tool, turning visitors into leads and leads into customers. From high-quality blog posts that attract organic traffic, to landing pages that capture leads, to sales pages that close deals, your website plays a major role in every step of your marketing funnel.

The importance of a website goes beyond marketing, too. It's an incredibly effective tool for business operations. From offering instant customer service through live chat features to simplifying the sales process with automated checkouts, websites can streamline many aspects of your business, freeing up time and resources for growth.

But perhaps the most vital role a website plays is in building trust and credibility. In today's digital era, customers expect businesses to have an online presence. A professional, user-friendly website conveys the message that you are a trustworthy, legitimate business. It reassures customers that you're not just real, but reliable and invested in their experience.

Without a website, you miss the chance to tell your brand's story in your own words. A well-crafted 'About Us' page, for instance, can communicate your values, mission, and passion to your customers, helping them feel a personal connection with your brand. Sharing your story sparks emotion, builds trust and turns casual visitors into passionate brand advocates.

In the world of online retail, your website works hard for you, serving as a salesperson that never sleeps. It displays your products or services, explains their benefits, and makes the purchasing process seamless. Packed with persuasive sales copy, high-quality images, and compelling calls to action, your website can be your most powerful sales tool.

The role of a website in online marketing cannot be understated. It anchors all your marketing efforts, from SEO to email marketing to social media promotion. Each of these marketing channels directs potential customers back to your website.

It's also worth noting that a website offers long-term value. Once it's set up, the ongoing costs are typically low compared to other marketing expenses. And over time, as you build up valuable content and generate more organic search traffic, your website can become an ongoing source of new leads and customers.

In conclusion, a website sits at the epicenter of your online business. Its importance extends beyond its role as a digital storefront or a marketing tool. It is your space on the internet, one that you control and shape to reflect your brand and meet your business goals. It is, in essence, the heart of your online presence and marketing strategy.

Chapter 3: Marketing Funnels

Imagine a funnel. It's wider at the top and narrows down as it descends. This succinctly alludes to the concept of marketing funnels, the third prong of our online business suite. In essence, a marketing funnel is a strategic approach that enables you to guide potential customers from the point of first interaction down to the final purchase. This funnel comprises various stages – awareness, consideration, conversion, retention, and advocacy. Each stage requires a different approach but is equally vital. You create awareness about your products or services and engage the audience's interest. The consideration stage involves presenting potential buyers with relevant information that helps them evaluate your offer. In the conversion phase, you convert prospects into paying customers. Post-purchase, you focus on retention strategies to foster repeat business. Lastly, the advocacy phase turns your customers into brand ambassadors. Understanding the anatomy of the marketing funnel is your ticket to maximizing online sales.

What is a Marketing Funnel?

A marketing funnel, also known as a sales funnel or a purchasing funnel, is a model that illustrates the journey potential customers take from first becoming aware of your brand to ultimately making a purchase. It's essential to understand that it presents more than a simple guideline for sales. It's a roadmap of the customer experience, from initial brand discovery to loyal customer and brand advocate.

The marketing funnel allows you to understand and anticipate patterns in consumer behavior. By intuitively knowing where a prospect is in the funnel, you can streamline your communication strategies to meet their needs at every point. In doing so, you optimally lead them towards the final stages of making a purchase and beyond.

The concept of a marketing funnel can be traced back to 1898 when Elias St. Elmo Lewis developed the AIDA model, which includes Awareness, Interest, Desire, and Action stages. Over time, this model has been refined and expanded into what we now call the marketing funnel.

The aim of a marketing funnel is to attract the highest number of potential customers (also known as leads) and gradually guide them towards purchasing a product or service, turning them from potential customers to actual buyers. The funnel shape represents the fact that a large number of potential customers get filtered down to a smaller number of actual customers who complete the buying process.

When conceived strategically, the marketing funnel serves as the backbone of an effective marketing plan. It connects all of your marketing efforts and helps you evaluate each one's effectiveness by defining crucial points in the consumer's journey, where you can track metrics and define success.

But the marketing funnel isn't just about getting people to buy from you — it also takes into consideration building and maintaining relationships with customers post-purchase. It emphasizes the importance of adding value to the customer at each stage and nurturing a relationship that will stimulate future purchases. It is here where the concepts of customer retention and brand advocacy come into play.

An effective marketing funnel is also flexible and dynamic, continually evolving to meet the changing needs and behaviors of customers. As such, it's not enough for businesses to set up a marketing funnel and leave it. Regular reviews and refinements are necessary to optimize its performance and remain attuned to shifting market trends and demands.

While the steps of the marketing funnel can slightly vary depending on the source, the conventional stages include: Awareness, Consideration, Conversion, Retention, and Advocacy. These stages succinctly express the customer's journey from the moment of first encountering your brand to the point of becoming an active promoter to others.

The marketing funnel not only aids in understanding the customer's journey but also clarifies the different types of content and messages that should be provided at each stage. In doing so, it helps businesses target their marketing tactics more effectively.

For you as a website owner, understanding and implementing a marketing funnel takes a bit of time, a bit of strategy and a bit of tech. But, the payoff of a carefully optimized funnel is precious: more leads, more conversions, and more growth for your business.

Ultimately, the marketing funnel is about focusing on the customer's journey and ensuring that you're meeting their needs at every stage. It's about providing value with each stage, which helps build trust and loyalty and ultimately leads to conversions.

By learning how to create a marketing funnel for your website, you will have a systematic process to turn potential visitors into loyal customers. So, get ready as you're about to step into an endeavor that can make a significant difference in your online business success.

By examining the behavior and decision-making process of your existing customers, you can gain valuable insights into how to optimize your marketing funnel. This data-driven approach can also help you identify bottlenecks or friction points that may be causing potential customers to exit the funnel before making a purchase.

So, now that we have an understanding of what a marketing funnel is, in the next chapters, we'll delve into its individual stages and discover the best practices to optimize them for maximum conversions and customer retention.

HOW MARKETING FUNNELS WORK

Continuing our exploration of marketing funnels, this section will delve into the nitty-gritty of how they operate. Understanding these operations is fundamental for any website owner aiming to drive sales and grow their online business through effective marketing strategies.

At its core, a marketing funnel represents the journey a potential customer takes from their first interaction with your brand until the point of purchase. Picture it as a funnel-shaped process, wide at the top, narrowing down towards the end. This visual metaphor represents the gradual filtering of a broad audience into a subset of customers.

A well-structured marketing funnel typically breaks down into five key stages. Each stage corresponds to a mindset or action step the customer needs to encounter to proceed down the funnel. These stages include: Awareness, Consideration, Conversion, Retention, and Advocacy.

Firstly, the Awareness stage marks the point where potential customers encounter your website or brand for the very first time. It may come through a marketing campaign, an online search, or word of mouth. The primary goal of this stage is to educate the potential customer about your brand and its offerings.

The next stage, Consideration, involves getting the already attracted leads to start deliberately thinking about your products or services. This stage involves delving deeper into the details about what your business provides, their benefits, and why they are the go-to solutions the potential customers need.

In the Conversion stage, potential customers decide whether or not to purchase what your website offers. This stage involves a finely-tuned combination of persuasive techniques, engaging content and compelling calls-to-action that nudge the customer towards making a purchase.

Just getting a customer to purchase your product or service doesn't mark the end of the journey, far from it. The Retention stage steps in here. Aim for repeat customers by nurturing an ongoing relationship. This could be achieved through regular communication via emails, special loyalty incentives, and continuously offering exceptional products and services.

Finally, the Advocacy stage is where customers love your products or services so much that they're willing to recommend them to others. Happy customers can become potent advocates for your brand, spreading their satisfaction through word of mouth or social media feedback.

It's important to note that not all website visitors will make it to the end of the marketing funnel. Depending on its efficiency and the nature of your business, only a smaller, meticulously-nurtured subset will become loyal customers and brand advocates. The challenge lies in maximizing this subset.

A marketing funnel works by systematically guiding the potential customer through a series of stages. Each stage careens attention away from every other distraction and centers their focus on one decision at a time. In short, it's a gradual conversion strategy that's built on the foundation of human psychology and the principles of persuasion.

In practice, the stages of a marketing funnel often overlap and aren't always as linear as it sounds. Depending on your marketing objectives and the nature of your products or services, you might need to adjust the process or include additional stages to fit your business model. But by understanding the central purpose of each stage, you can help guide your customers through their journey with more precision and influence, resulting in increased sales.

More appreciable, a marketing funnel allows you to measure the success of your marketing efforts. By tracking how many individuals proceed to each stage, you can pinpoint areas that may be lacking and adjust strategies accordingly to improve conversion rates.

So there you have it, a broad overview of how marketing funnels work. The subsequent sections of this book will delve deeper into each stage of the marketing funnel and provide you with detailed strategies on how to optimize each.

Awareness Stage After understanding the essence of marketing funnels, we are at the precipice of your potential customers' journey - the Awareness Stage. This part of your marketing funnel is undeniably crucial as it's often said you don't get a second chance to make a first impression. The objective here is two-fold: firstly, to capture their attention, and secondly, ensuring that it hooks them in further into the marketing funnel.

The awareness stage is the topmost part of the funnel and is where potential customers first come into contact with your brand. More often than not, these individuals are seeking solutions or answers to a challenge or problem that your products or services could address. Therefore, it's key to ensure the content you present leaves an immediate, positive impact, and sparks their curiosity. On-site content such as blog posts, guides, and videos can serve as valuable sources of information that start to establish trust and authority in your industry. However, it's equally important to remember that selling is not the aim of this stage - it's all about delivering value.

But how do you reach these potential customers in the first place? A variety of channels can be used to amplify your reach including organic search, social media, advertising and promotional efforts, and even word-of-mouth. Moreover, these channels act as gateways for these individuals to discover your brand and consequently, your website. Therefore, how your brand is portrayed, along with the value proposition of your content, will determine the level of interest generated and can make a significant difference in the number of users who progress to the next stage of your marketing funnel - the Consideration Stage.

Consideration Stage Once your customer has established a sense of mindfulness about your service or product (thanks to the earlier stage known as the awareness stage), it's now time to navigate smoothly into the all-important 'Consideration Stage.' This marketing funnel phase is where potential customers start weighing their options, making comparisons, and seriously considering your product or service as a potential solution to their identified need or want.

It's crucial, during this stage, to provide detailed information that makes your product or service stand out among the competition. Explain why your brand is unique, accentuating its superior features, benefits, and overall value. You can execute this effectively through diverse content forms like more in-depth blog posts, explainer videos, podcasts, webinars, and case studies. However, remember not to pressure your potential customer into buying now. At this stage, they're more interested in learning and comparing, so let hard sell tactics take a back seat to providing valuable, decision-supporting information.

Moreover, consider creating personalized customer experiences at this stage. Utilize data you've gathered during the awareness stage to understand your potential customers better and provide them with tailor-made interactions. This consideration stage is an excellent opportunity to start fostering relationships and building trust with your potential customers, preparing a solid foundation for the subsequent conversion stage. Note that each stage should flow seamlessly into the next — subtle yet persuasive, nudging your potential customer closer to the much-desired sale!

Conversion Stage is where your prospects decide to take action and become a paying customer. The act of converting can take on various forms - from purchasing a product, signing up for a membership, or contracting for a service. It's the critical juncture where the relationship between your business and the customer is defined and where revenue is principally generated.

At the conversion stage, your persuasive techniques need to be at their strongest. After initiating awareness and piquing the prospect's interest during the previous phases, now is the time to make a convincing case to the potential customers that your product or service is the ultimate solution to their problem. You've got to demonstrate the tangible value and undeniable benefits that they stand to gain from their investment in your business. This can be achieved through compelling sales pages, convincing conversations during sales calls, or alluring automated email sequences. The aim is to nudge the already engaged leads into making a decision by showcasing the superiority of your offerings over any competitors.

Remember, not every single person who arrives at this stage will make a purchase, and that's perfectly alright. The Conversion Stage isn't when the journey of every lead comes to a successful end; rather, it's the crossroads where leads who are genuinely interested in your offerings become customers. Every effort should be made to make this transition as seamless and straightforward as possible. Clear pricing information, diverse payment options, and an easy checkout process can make all the difference. At the end of the day, the Conversion Stage is about sealing the deal; it's about transforming the interest you've carefully cultivated into concrete sales. It's seemingly simple but vastly influential in your business success.

Retention Stage Following the conversion stage, the customer now enters the pivotal retention phase. This is the stage where your focus shifts from acquiring customers to keeping them engaged and satisfied with the value of your product or service. At this point, your clients have already made their purchase and experienced your product or service. Now, it's time to make sure they stick around. Remember, it's always less expensive to retain an existing customer than it is to acquire a new one, thereby making retention a critical part of the marketing funnel.

In the retention stage, you need to continue providing value and fostering the relationships you've built with your customers. This could involve offering exceptional customer support, providing additional educational content, or introducing loyalty programs or incentives. You can use methods like email marketing or social media engagement to keep your brand at the forefront of their minds. Take advantage of any opportunity to make your existing customers feel special and appreciated. Remember, satisfied customers can become your best brand advocates.

Moreover, it's worth noting that the retention stage offers a prime opportunity for upselling and cross-selling to your existing clients. Since you have already built trust and credibility with your customers, you can introduce additional products or services that can further fulfill their needs. Be sure these offerings genuinely add value to your customers' experience, and aren't just an attempt to squeeze out more revenue. The key aspect to keep in mind through the retention stage is that customer satisfaction leads to customer loyalty, and a loyal customer base is a strong foundation for the long-term success of your online business.

Advocacy Stage is centered around transforming your customers into devoted promoters of your brand. After building a trust-filled relationship with your customers during the retention stage, you can now influence them to turn around and advocate for your services or products. This stage is the pinnacle of customer satisfaction and loyalty, where customers so delighted with your offerings vigorously promote your website to others. Their positive testimonials and word-of-mouth referrals are powerful tools that can significantly impact your business's growth and success.

Your goal in this stage is to facilitate and encourage this advocacy. Start by providing offer referrals or loyalty programs that reward your customers for promoting your business. By incentivizing this promotion, you can convert regular customers into zealous brand ambassadors. The discounts, freebies, or exclusive content you offer in return for referrals not only spur advocacy actions but also reinforce customer loyalty.

It's important as well to engage customers on multiple channels. Encourage customers to post reviews on your website, share your content on social media, or write about their positive experiences in their personal blogs. You can also provide social-proof features on your website or social media platforms where customers can share their testimonies. It's essential to remember that in this advocacy stage, the goal is to not only keep customers coming back for more but to get them to spread the word about your business. Thus, turning your customers into advocates helps maximize the return on your marketing investment, deepening your relationships with customers and expanding your reach to new potentials.

Chapter 4: Building Your Website

Now that we've acquired a solid understanding of marketing funnels, let's shift our focus to the heart of your online enterprise - your website. First off, it's crucial to pick the right platform that not only aligns with your technical prowess but also caters to your specific business needs. It can be an all-in-one platform that handles everything from hosting to webpage design, or a more hands-on CMS where you can wield greater control over your website's functionality and aesthetics. Once this foundation is established, we delve into the essential elements of a high converting website. The design and layout of your website must induce simplicity, usability, and a visual appeal that aligns with your brand image. Next, we talk about crafting compelling web content that syncs with the customer's journey in the marketing funnel. This is where you'll learn to create and optimize content that triggers interest, establishes authority, and promotes interaction. Lastly, the importance of SEO cannot be stressed enough. It's an integral tool that ensures your website gets the visibility it deserves on search engine results, driving organic traffic that is crucial for the growth of your online venture. It's a lot to take in, but remember – a well-designed, content-rich, and SEO-optimized website paves the way for a successful marketing funnel.

Choosing the Right Platform

As we delve further into the finer details of creating a functional, sales-maximizing website, we meet a significant decision: the selection of our website platform. It's essential to understand that your website is an integral part of your marketing funnel. Therefore, settling for the appropriate platform warrants careful consideration.

There is a multitude of platforms available today, each offering its unique features, advantages, and potential drawbacks. Your decision should hinge on your business's specific requirements, goals, and technical expertise, among other factors. Can you handle the trivial technicalities yourself, or do you need a user-friendly, seamless platform? Let's look at some highly recommended options to guide your decision-making process.

One popular platform that comes to mind is WordPress. This platform provides great flexibility and is relatively straightforward to use, even for beginners. Yet, it offers robust, advanced features for those willing to delve a bit deeper. It has a vast library of plug-ins and themes, and it facilitates SEO integration, making it easier to attract and retain your target market. A particularly convenient feature is its compatibility with a vast pool of third-party tools that can fortify your marketing funnel.

Next, we have Shopify, your go-to platform if your business is heavily geared towards e-commerce. Adaptability is what sets Shopify apart. You can sell both digital and physical products or services, all in a speedy and secure manner. Shopify's built-in SEO features and ability to integrate with social media platforms only amplify your reach, bringing more individuals through your marketing funnel.

Squarespace is another reputable platform fit for businesses seeking an exquisite visual presence without the heavy lifting of learning code. It is a platform well-suited for individuals who want to focus heavily on the design aspect. Also, with robust SEO tools and the ability to integrate with other marketing platforms, it can contribute significantly towards your marketing funnel effectiveness.

Wix is another platform that offers a unique blend of user-friendly design tools and SEO prowess. With a drag-and-drop interface and hundreds of pre-made templates, creating a beautifully designed website without advanced technical knowledge has never been easier.

Lastly, Magento, a platform pretty popular among well-established e-commerce businesses, generally requires a higher level of technical knowledge due to its robust and complex feature set. Yet, its ability to support large-scale e-commerce operations makes it a strong contender.

How do you choose from these options? Begin by assessing your needs. What's the nature of your business? What's your level of technical expertise? As we have seen, a platform like Magento, though robust, may pose unnecessary difficulties for a small-scale e-commerce startup, whereas a platform like Shopify could provide a much smoother ride.

If you're non-technical or on a tight budget, choosing a platform that allows you to create a website without writing a single line of code can be a game-changer. Platforms like Wix or Squarespace provide such user-friendly interfaces.

Another worthy point to consider is the adaptability of the platform. Can it smoothly accommodate future growth? After all, your business won't be stagnant; neither should your website. Look out for platforms that allow you to scale effectively and efficiently.

SEO capabilities are another factor you can't afford to ignore. Remember, your website platform's SEO integrations will significantly influence your website's visibility. Platforms like WordPress and Shopify have got you covered here with their substantial built-in SEO features.

Also, take a close look at the pricing before deciding. Some platforms offer a lot of value at a minimum cost, while others might seem cost-effective initially but impose additional charges for essential features. Carefully analyze what features you're getting at what price and budget wisely.

Customer support is another aspect to consider. Whether you're a technical person or not, you might require help at some point. Check out reviews about the customer service of these platforms. Are they available 24/7? Do they respond promptly and effectively?

Finally, and quite importantly, ensure that the potential platform integrates well with the other tools and applications you plan to use. Synchronization amongst your tools is key to maintaining a smooth, effective marketing funnel.

Having said this, there is no one-size-fits-all platform. It's a highly personalized decision based on your requirements, goals, budget, and skills. Embark on careful analysis, weigh your options critically, and make an informed decision that underpins the success of your entire marketing funnel.

Essential Elements of a High Converting Website

With a clear understanding of the context, we will now delve into the critical components that can make your website a highly converting platform. Just like a well-oiled machine, every part of your website should work harmoniously towards achieving one goal - maximizing conversions. Below are the necessary elements of a high-converting website that, when implemented correctly, can steer your online business towards unparalleled success.

First, let's talk about your website's design and feel. In the digital realm, your website serves as your storefront. If it's visually unappealing or tough to navigate, visitors can lose interest and leave, which is the exact opposite of what you want. It should be professional, inviting, and a reflection of your brand. It should also be easy to navigate, with an intuitive interface where your potential customers can find what they need without any struggle.

Secondly, your website's loading speed significantly influences your visitors' user experience. If your site takes too long to load, you risk losing potential customers, as people typically have a short tolerance for slow-loading websites. There are numerous tools available online to help you analyze and improve your website's loading speed.

Thirdly, mobile optimization is no longer just an option but a necessity. With a large chunk of internet users browsing via their mobile devices, your website must be responsive and should adjust seamlessly to different screen sizes. Failure to optimize your website for mobile users will lead to a poor user experience and, consequently, lower conversions.

The use of powerful headlines is another essential element. They serve as the first point of interaction with your visitors, and thus, must be captivating enough to hook them and make them want to stay longer on your website.

There's also the need for strong, persuasive calls-to-action (CTAs). A CTA is an instruction to your audience designed to provoke an immediate response - it could be "Buy Now!", "Sign Up!", or "Learn More!". CTAs should be strategically placed and should stand out from the rest of the content.

An element often overlooked is trust signals. These could be in the form of testimonials, reviews, or security badges. They can greatly help to alleviate the doubts in your visitor's mind and convert them into customers.

The quality of your images and videos can also make or break your website. They should be of high-resolution, appealing, and relevant to your product or service. Low-quality media can make your brand appear unprofessional and turn off potential customers.

Content remains king in the digital world. Apart from engaging graphics, you need to provide compelling and valuable content. It should answer your visitors' questions, solve their problems, and position you as an authority in your industry. Remember, it's not just about selling, it's about providing value.

Your website's contact information should be easy to locate. If visitors can't easily find how to contact you, they may become frustrated and leave. More than that, it's mandatory to have a privacy policy to exhibit transparency and build trust with your visitors. Clear and comprehensive privacy policies assure visitors that their information is safe with you.

A live chat feature on your website can make a significant difference. When visitors have queries or concerns, they prefer getting immediate answers. A live chat feature provides real-time support and can lead to increased customer satisfaction and higher conversions.

Besides, you should have a clear path in your navigation for visitors to become customers. It could be a simple journey from the landing page to the product page, to the checkout page. If your website's sales funnel is confusing or convoluted, visitors may lose patience and abandon their purchase.

An analytics tool to track your website's performance is also crucial. It helps collect key data on visitor behavior, traffic sources, popular pages, and more. You can use these insights to make data-driven decisions to optimize your website for higher conversions.

Finally, remember that a high-converting website is always a work in progress. Given the dynamic nature of the online marketplace, it's essential to keep iterating and improving your website based on industry trends, customer feedback, and performance analysis. The key lies in continuous testing, learning, and optimizing.

Shortly, we will take a more comprehensive look at the website design and layout, creating compelling web content, and the importance of SEO. Brace yourself to uncover the nitty-gritty of building your high-converting website!

Website Design and Layout is an essential aspect of a high-performing online marketing funnel. The design and layout of your website can determine whether a visitor stays and explores or leaves and never comes back. At the core, your website should be visually pleasing, intuitive, and responsive across different devices. A cluttered website with subpar user experience can deter potential customers, negatively impacting your conversion rates.

The layout of your website should guide visitors effortlessly through your marketing funnel. The end goal is getting the visitor to take the action you desire, whether that's purchasing a product, signing up for a newsletter, or contacting your team. To achieve this, consider applying the rule of thirds in your design plan. This principle involves dividing your webpage into thirds, horizontally and vertically, resulting in a grid. The objective is to place essential components or calls to action at the intersections of this grid, usually where the eyes naturally gravitate.

Moreover, the choice of colors, fonts, and images is paramount, as these elements speak volumes about your brand and aid in influencing user behavior. Use colors purposefully, understanding the psychological effect they may have on your visitors. Fonts should be reader-friendly, aiming for readability and legibility over stylistic choices. Clear, well-crafted images can convey messages faster than text and contribute to the overall aesthetic appeal of your website. Remember, your site isn't just about looking pretty; it's about driving visitors down the marketing funnel towards conversion.

Creating Compelling Web Content sits at the heart of your digital marketing. Enhanced quality and relevant web content will attract new visitors, engage them and help build trust. Yet, constructing said content requires a clear understanding of your audience's needs, your business goals, and unveiling the connection between them.

A robust content strategy begins with understanding your target audience and identifying how your website can fulfill their needs. Each piece of content should be designed to help your potential customers achieve their goals or solve a problem. This strategy is not merely about being informative but also about being captivating. Use engaging adjectives, tell stories, discuss pain points on what your audience can relate to. It helps users understand what benefits they can get from your product or service, and thus progresses them further down the marketing funnel.

Furthermore, it's essential to think about the structure and format of your content. The text should be scannable with headings, subheadings, bullet points, and short paragraphs to maintain the readability score high.

Include engaging visuals; images, infographics, videos to keep visitors engaged & feel connected. Also, it's crucial to keep the content fresh and updated, ensure a regular publishing schedule to keep the visitors coming back (retention) and become a resource for your industry (advocacy). After all, creating compelling web content is about fostering and maintaining relationships with your platform's visitors, leading to increased conversions and business growth.

Importance of SEO. Following compelling content creation and sketching out a keenly designed website, one cannot stress enough the significance of SEO, or Search Engine Optimization. SEO is the critical gear in the engine of your online business. It may appear invisible on the surface, but its workings drive the functionality of your website, ensuring its visibility. In the ocean of the internet, SEO is the lighthouse that guides your prospective customers to your shores.

SEO is like your online megaphone. It amplifies your message to reach those who are seeking precisely what you offer. How so? Through targeted keywords. Whether your website sells rainbow-colored umbrellas or provides holistic health coaching, there are specific phrases and words your target demographic keys into search engines. By strategically integrating these keywords into your web content, you increase your website's visibility on search engine results pages, making your site easier to discover by your desired clientele.

It's not just about visibility, though. SEO also works to enhance user experience. Nothing's more frustrating for a customer than a slow-loading webpage or a disorganized site structure. Good SEO incorporates clean coding, efficient website design, and mindful structuring to reduce page load times, eliminate errors, and streamline navigation, respectively. If you're looking to keep your marketing funnel fluid, SEO is the liquid gold that lubricates its every corner. It directs, it enhances, and it optimizes your online presence, effectively bridging the gap between your products or services and the customers who need them.

Chapter 5: Creating Your Marketing Funnel

Kicking off the creation of your marketing funnel begins with a deep, crisp understanding of your target market. Consider their needs, preferences, and motivations. This will help in crafting attraction strategies tailored to ignite their interest and curiosity. The creation of valuable content serves as a lighthouse, drawing your potential customers closer. Additionally, your social media platforms serve not just as broadcasting towers for your content but also as engagement hubs where you create conversations and cultivate digital relationships. Remember though, any relationship thrives with constant communication. That's where email marketing steps in, keeping your audience updated and interested through a steady flow of personalized communication. Cumulatively, these elements act as the gravitational force pulling potential customers into your orbit and keeping them there - a well-oiled, dynamic marketing funnel, tailored to be the right match for your online business model.

Define Your Target Market

Before diving into the practical strategies and metrics of setting up your marketing funnel, it's crucial to start by knowing your target market. Understanding the people you aim to serve with your products or services isn't merely beneficial. It's essential. It will influence each step of your marketing funnel - from the content you create to the channels you select for promotion.

First, you have to grasp what a target market is. It pertains to a well-defined group of potential consumers that a business aims to serve. It could be a mixture of attributes including age, gender, location, occupation, income level, lifestyle, and personal preferences. The more specific this is, the better you can tailor and perfect your messaging to resonate with this specific audience.

By understanding your optimal customer, you will be positioned to discover where they are likely to be online, what content they engage with, and what products or services they are possibly interested in. Essentially, defining your target market is about identifying and understanding the 'who', 'what', 'where', 'why', and 'how' of your potential customers.

Determining your target market isn't just about knowing who your customers are on a demographic level, but it also includes understanding them on a psychographic level. Psychographics assess attitudes, aspirations, interests, lifestyle, and other psychological factors. It gives you deeper insight into your customers' behaviors and motivations than demographics alone.

One of the best places to start when defining your target market is by checking out your competitors. See who they are targeting and how they do it. But remember, it's not about copying what they do, but leveraging this information to better your own strategies. This competitor analysis can help generate a clearer perspective of your own potential customer base.

Another starting point is to review your existing customer base if you have one. Study the characteristics of your best customers, those who buy the most, or who have a high level of engagement. Look for common attributes amongst them, as these could provide valuable insights into who your future efforts should focus on.

You may also find it beneficial to create hypothetical buyer personas. These personas are detailed descriptions of an idealized customer, a model representative of your target market. They serve as a guide to help you better understand who you are marketing to. But remember, these personas should be data-driven and realistic, not based on assumptions.

When creating these personas, go beyond the age, income, and occupation, consider things like what challenges they face or what they value. Look into their goals and how your product or service could help them achieve those. Find out what information they need to make a purchase. Understanding these details will allow you to create a robust and personalized marketing funnel.

Once you have formulated your buyer personas, you can then start tailoring the elements of your marketing funnel. This includes creating content that resonates with them, targeting them on the platforms where they spend their time and structuring your products, services, or offers to best meet their discerned needs and wants.

It's also imperative to remember that target markets can evolve. That's why it's essential to revisit and revise your target market periodically. Consumer habits change, as do market trends, so ensure your target market and buyer persona descriptions remain applicable.

At its core, your target market is the most likely group of consumers to purchase from you. Understanding them on a deep level allows your marketing message to be more precise, personal and effective — which ultimately leads to a higher likelihood of conversion. The more data you can collect about your target customers, the more able you are to deliver relevant messaging that resonates, enables your brand to connect, and ultimately attracts more leads into your marketing funnel.

Defining your target market may seem like a large task to undertake, but the rewards are immense. By knowing your prospective customers intimately, you can fine-tune your marketing messages, convert more visitors into leads, and ultimately, achieve higher sales. So, take the time now to gain a deep understanding of your target market, cultivate the skill of seeing the world from their perspective, and curate your offerings to serve their needs.

In a nutshell, to build a marketing funnel that maximizes your sales, you need to start with a clearly defined target market. This foundation will guide all your marketing strategies through the funnel stages outlined in the following sections and enable you to hit the right audience at the right time with the right message.

ATTRACTION STRATEGIES

The next critical component in building a successful marketing funnel is, without a doubt, the implementation of effective attraction strategies. These are methodically planned tactics that aim to pull your target audience into the mechanism of your marketing funnel. The overall objective is to create interest and curiosity, thereby driving people to explore, engage with, and eventually invest in your product or service. Let's delve into some high-yielding strategies.

Creating Valuable Content is an art unto itself, interwoven with strategy, psychology, and mindfulness of your audience's needs. When your content is valuable, it accomplishes several things. It answers your audience's questions, establishes your brand's expertise in the industry, grows organic traffic through SEO, and converts visitors into leads which are steps further into your marketing funnel.

The key to creating this value lies in understanding your audience thoroughly. Get into their heads: what are their pain points? What solutions are they seeking? What language resonates with them? Direct your content towards answering these questions. Use analytics tools to reveal what content types and topics your audience engages with most. Employ that data to tailor your creative process and ensure that your output is always aligned with your audience's desires. Always remember, content created without the reader in mind ends up serving no one.

Additionally, embrace a variety of formats. Blog posts, how-to guides, ebooks, webinars, infographics, podcasts, videos - each of these has the potential to reach different segments of your audience, keeping the content fresh and engaging. But, authenticity is important too. "One size fits all" does not work here. Customize each piece for its respective platform in terms of length, tone and style. Lastly, remember the SEO. Proper use of keywords, meta tags, and backlinks can potentially increase your visibility across search engines, driving high-quality organic traffic to your site. So, with a solid understanding of your audience, a commitment to rich, authentic offerings, and a robust SEO strategy, you're equipped to craft the valuable content your marketing funnel needs.

Social Media Marketing can be a game-changer for your online business if done strategically. Social media platforms like Facebook, Instagram, LinkedIn, Twitter, and others have become pivotal in creating a robust online presence and engaging effectively with your target audience. Leveraging these platforms will help you reach out to a global audience, enhance brand visibility, and build a solid marketing funnel for your business.

Primarily, social media marketing starts with identifying your audience. It's crucial to understand who your target customers are, their interests, and where they spend their time online. Only by knowing your audience well enough can you engage them with meaningful and engaging content that resonates with them. Stellar content is one aspect that can't be compromised; this can range from informative blogs, visually appealing infographics, relevant videos, to attention-grabbing posts. Sharing your content across diverse social media channels will boost your brand recognition and turn your visitors into potential leads. Be consistent with your content strategy, and remember, it's all about offering value to your audience.

Another essential factor of social media marketing is engaging with your followers. Direct engagement will not only make your customers feel valued but also strengthen your relationship with them - encouraging customer loyalty. A common way of engaging is by responding to comments, messages, reviews, or questions promptly. Asking for their feedback, conducting polls, or simply thanking them for their support can build a positive rapport. You can also run contests or promotional campaigns to engage your followers and increase brand awareness. In turn, this active engagement will help you navigate your audience seamlessly through your marketing funnel, leading to maximum conversions. Thus, social media marketing is a comprehensive step in creating a successful marketing funnel.

Email Marketing is a classic, yet undeniably effective form of connecting with potential customers. Its usage has evolved over the years, shifting from being used for mass, untargeted broadcasts to a carefully strategized component of a successful marketing funnel. Emails give you a much-awaited chance to tell your brand's story, share useful information, and deliver promotional offers all in one go. Moreover, it's a zero-cost interaction which increases its efficiency in the cost-to-result ratio.

The effectiveness of email marketing lies in its ability to nurture leads. Remember, everyone on your email list has expressed a level of interest in your business, that's presuming you've compiled your list ethically. They've signed up because they're intrigued by your products or services, and that's an excellent starting point. Your role is to keep their interest piqued and usher them through your funnel stages. Through various professionally composed emails, such as newsletters, promotional offers, and alerts for new blog posts or product launches, you keep your audience engaged and privy to what's new with your business.

Personalization is key in email marketing. It's not about bombarding your potential customers with emails. It's about understanding your clients' individual needs and preferences and delivering content that's tailored to them. Email segmentation can help with this, allowing you to group your subscribers based on their interests, purchase history, and how they interacted with your website. Crafting customized emails for these segmented groups lead to more engagement, which could translate into more conversions. Remember, the goal isn't just to keep them interested, but to ultimately guide them to making a purchase decision. In the next section, we will discuss how you can turn these engaged visitors into promising leads.

Chapter 6: Implementing Your Marketing Funnel

Following up on creating your marketing funnel in the previous chapter, you're now at a stage where you must meticulously implement it. This is a pivotal chapter where you'll learn about transforming your website's visitors into valuable leads. This process entails crafting high-converting landing pages that captivate potential leads and offering irresistible lead magnets that can motivate them into sharing their contact information. Once you have their information, the objective then changes to turning these leads into bonafide customers. This transition is facilitated by using automated email marketing campaigns to nurture your leads, well-structured sales pages that artfully guide your customer towards making purchase decisions, and employing reliable payment gateways to smooth out the transaction process. Each of these steps are crucial to implementing your marketing funnel effectively, and we're going to delve deeper into these tactics, exploring best practices and strategies to ensure your funnel operates like a well-oiled machine. Combining the wisdom of our own experience, with the proven methods from industry giants, this chapter will give you the arsenal to implement a potent marketing funnel that is primed to maximize your sales.

Turning Visitors into Leads

In the journey of a potential customer through your marketing funnel, the first step is attracting them to your website. But the big question is, once they have landed on your website, how do you turn these visitors into proper leads? This process of capturing customer interest in a product or service for the purpose of developing a sales pipeline is what this section is all about. Here, we'll dive into the strategies needed to effectively turn your website visitors into leads, a vital component for the success of any online business.

Remember, a lead is a visitor who has shown interest in your product or service by giving you their information. But you can't simply expect someone to come to your website and hand over their info. You have to give them a reason. That's where landing pages and lead magnets come in. They're the tools you'll utilize to provide the incentive needed to encourage information sharing.

Landing Pages. A landing page is a page on your website where you direct your traffic, with the aim of achieving a certain action from the visitor. Whether that be signing up for a newsletter, downloading an e-book, or registering for a free trial, these actions result in visitors becoming leads. How? By requiring the visitor to fill in their personal information in order to complete the action. This gives you their contact information for future communication opportunities.

Designing effective landing pages is key here. First and foremost, the landing page should clearly display the value proposition. This is what sets you apart from the competition. It's what draws the visitor in and convinces them that it's worth entering their personal information. The design should also be clean and non-distracting. The goal is to funnel visitors toward that one specific action, so any other distracting elements can hamper your conversion rate.

Your landing page should include an enticing call-to-action (CTA). The CTA basically guides your visitors towards the desired action you want them to take. It should be clear, concise and persuasive. Also, optimize your forms by asking for just the amount of information you truly need. If you request too many details, you may scare off potential leads.

Lead Magnets. Now let's talk about lead magnets. The term 'lead magnet' might sound a bit technical, but it's rather simple. Essentially, a lead magnet is something of value that you offer to your visitors for free in exchange for their contact information.

A lead magnet can be a discount, a free trial, an e-book, a webinar, or even an exclusive piece of content. The important thing is for it to be valuable enough to your visitors that they're willing to provide their personal details to get it. It's a win-win scenario -- your visitor gets something of value and you get their contact information, turning them into a lead.

To create a successful lead magnet, think about the challenges, problems, and needs of your target audience. The lead magnet should offer a solution or resource that helps them in some way. Also, remember to keep it relevant to your services or products. Giving away a free ebook about gardening, for example, won't be much use if you're primarily selling sporting goods.

Combining an effective landing page and a compelling lead magnet is a proven strategy to turn visitors into leads. However, there is an underlying factor you need to consider: trust. Visitors will only give you their personal information if they trust your site. Ensure your website and the landing page look professional and trustworthy. Having testimonials from previous customers can greatly boost your credibility and increase your conversion rates.

Furthermore, remember that turning visitors into leads is a crucial step in the marketing funnel, but it doesn't end there. The nurturing must continue in the next stages of the funnel to eventually turn these leads into loyal, paying customers.

Also, remember to continually optimize your landing pages and lead magnets. Measure their effectiveness in terms of lead generation, and tweak them as necessary to achieve the best results. A/B testing is a great way to identify what works best for your audience. We will dive deeper into this in the 'Optimizing Your Marketing Funnel' section.

That's it for turning visitors into leads. Next, we'll discuss how to nurture those leads into becoming paying customers for your business.

Landing Pages are the crux of your marketing funnel, operating as a critical point of engagement with potential leads. For a marketing funnel to perform seamlessly, the creation of high-quality, user-friendly landing pages is absolutely vital. To put it simply, these pages are the ones your potential customers will 'land on,' following their interaction with one of your marketing efforts, such as clicking on an ad or a link in an email. The effectiveness of your landing pages has a direct impact on your conversion rate — they are, after all, the first taste your potential customers get of your offerings.

Landing pages must be designed with a cleverly strategic approach. It's not simply about making them look appealing, though that is surely one aspect of it. More importantly, they should be designed to guide visitors toward taking a specific action. This can range from making a purchase, signing up for an email newsletter, downloading a piece of content, or any other action that aligns with your marketing goals. Every element on the page — from the headline and body text to images, call-to-action buttons, and color schemes — should work in harmony to guide the visitor towards that action.

The devil is often in the details on these pages. For instance, your headline should directly relate to the ad or email that brought the visitor to the page, maintaining consistency and setting appropriate expectations. The copy should not just be persuasive, but also straightforward and concise, clearly communicating the benefits of taking the proposed action. The design and layout should be clean and intuitive, making the page easy to navigate. A strong, visible call to action (CTA) button is crucial, and even its color and placement can greatly influence conversion rates. Remember to limit the number of options available to the visitor. Instead, funnel them toward your desired action and eliminate potential distractions. By mastering these details, you can create landing pages that truly power your marketing funnel, turning casual visitors into engaged leads and, eventually, into customers.

Turning Leads into Customers

After leveraging your efforts on creating a captivating website and generating traffic, you're now enjoying a steady stream of leads coming in. That's fantastic. But leads alone aren't enough. Ultimately, your goal is to convert these leads into customers. How are you to make this vital leap? This section will guide you on how to turn curious visitors into paying customers through email automation, sales pages, and payment gateways.

Email Automation. One of the most effective tools in nurturing your leads into customers is email automation. Timing and content are the critical elements. You have to provide the right content to the right lead at the right time. And this can be a complicated task if done manually, especially when dealing with hundreds or thousands of leads. That's where email automation comes into the picture.

Email automation allows you to send personalized and relevant emails to your leads based on their actions and interactions with your website. For instance, if a lead downloads a specific guide from your page, automation can trigger a follow-up email relating to the guide's topic. By doing so, you are creating a more personalized experience which can, in turn, improve conversion rates.

Sales Pages. When you've nurtured your leads through automated emails and they've shown a significant interest in your product or service, you can then lead them to your sales page. A sales page is designed specifically to convince leads of the value of your offering and encourage a purchase.

Your sales page should be crafted thoughtfully and strategically. It needs to clearly articulate what the product or service is, why it's beneficial, and how it will resolve the potential customer's problem or meet their need. Include testimonials or case studies to lend more credibility and to showcase the results others achieved using your product or service.

Remember, you're not just listing facts about your product or service. You're telling a story. You're painting a picture of what the potential customer's life could be like with your product or service in it. Create a narrative that speaks directly to your audience, stirs their emotions, and prompts them to take action.

Payment Gateways. So, your leads are now convinced of the value you're offering and are ready to become customers. The last hurdle to clear in turning your leads into customers would be to facilitate a seamless payment process. The more frictionless the payment process is, the more likely leads will complete their purchase and convert into customers.

To achieve this, integrate reliable and known payment gateways into your website. These platforms not only make transactions quick and pain-free but also ensure that sensitive information is secure. When leads are confident about the security and efficiency of your payment process, their hesitations can be quelled, bringing them closer to becoming customers.

Popular options to consider include PayPal, Stripe, and Square. The key is to choose one that works best for your offering and your customers. Consider factors such as transaction fees, user interface, customer support, and geographical coverage.

Lastly, ensure that the checkout process is as streamlined as possible. Eliminate unnecessary steps and keep the design clear and simple. Don't give your leads an excuse to abandon their cart at the last minute.

The Pivot. An essential fact to remember is that converting leads into customers doesn't end after the first purchase. Each customer can potentially provide repeat business and even lead to referrals if they are happy with your product or service. Therefore, in a way, the process of turning leads into customers is ongoing and requires constant attention and refinement.

Keep the lines of communication open through email follow-ups or special offers. Seek their feedback and learn from it. Keep them engaged with valuable content relative to their interests or the specific product they purchased.

Continually remind them of the value you offer, and show appreciation for their loyalty and patronage. Remember, a satisfied customer is a loyal customer, and loyal customers can often become brand ambassadors naturally.

Turning leads into customers is a delicate, nuanced process that requires a deep understanding of the lead's needs and desires. But with these tactics of email automation, sales pages, and payment gateways, you'll be well on your way to seeing an upswing in your conversions and overall sales. Don't get disheartened if you don't see immediate results. Keep refining your approach, and you'll see steady progress. It's an investment that is worthwhile.

Email Automation is an indispensable component in your marketing funnel, capable of turning leads into bona fide customers. It refers to the use of software that enables you to send automated emails to segments of your contact list based on their interactions with your brand. This orchestration of correspondence takes the guesswork out of communicating with your prospects, ensuring that the right message gets to the right person at the right time.

When a potential customer exhibits interest in your brand, be it by subscribing to your newsletter or downloading a free resource, you've acquired a lead. But, it's not time to celebrate sales just yet. This is where the power of automation comes in. Automated follow-up emails serve as the touchpoints that nudge your leads further down your marketing funnel. For instance, after a lead signs up for your newsletter, an automated system can send a gracious welcome email. This can be followed by a series of value-adding emails that gently guide the lead through the stages of your funnel.

Moreover, effective email automation requires keen attention to the personalization and timing of your emails. For the former, make use of the data you've gathered about your leads. This might be their name, their previous purchases, or each interaction with your brand thus far. As for timing, contemplate on your lead's journey through your funnel. Certain interactions such as checkout abandonments deserve immediate responses while others like the initial sign-ups can afford a little breathing space. Essentially, your email automation strategy should deliver contextually relevant content to your leads at an optimal pace, providing value without overwhelming them.

Sales Pages serve as your virtual store, where visitors make that critical decision to either proceed with a purchase or leave empty-handed. A well-designed sales page can significantly boost conversion rates, turning visitors into paying customers. It's not just about touting the features and benefits of your product or service, rather it's about compelling storytelling that resonates with your prospects' needs and wants.

Firstly, your sales page must have a captivating headline that grabs attention and piques curiosity. Make it clear, concise, and directly related to your product or service. Use strong, persuasive words that incite emotions. Secondly, craft compelling copy to present the benefits, not just the features of your product. The copy should speak to the customer's pain points and present your product as the solution. Consider using the voice of your happy customers. Customer testimonials and reviews are much more convincing in illustrating your offerings' value than any sales pitch you can craft.

Last but not least, each sales page should close with a clear, compelling call to action (CTA). This is the 'final push' that urges them to take the desired action whether it be to purchase, sign up, or download. Avoid generic phrases like 'click here' as your CTA. Instead, employ specific, actionable language that is linked with the benefit, like 'sign up to get your free eBook' or 'buy now and save 20%.' Above all, understand that your sales pages are not just about selling. They are about imprinting your brand in the minds of the visitors, creating a relationship, and ensuring they will continue to return. Keep it congruent with your overall site aesthetics and brand messaging for a seamless customer journey.

Payment Gateways are an integral part of your online sales process. Imagine your website as a physical store - a payment gateway functions as your cashier. It's a digital tool that authorizes and processes transactions between your website and the customer's payment method. Your payment gateway is going to interact with credit card companies, banks, and other payment providers to finalize the transaction, ensuring that the money securely transfers from the customer's account into yours. Selecting the right one is crucial, as it directly affects your sales conversions.

Consider customer trust, reliability, ease of integration, and cost when selecting a payment gateway. Customers want to know that their private financial information remains secure, so it's wise to select a gateway that's known and trusted. Gateways such as PayPal, Stripe, and Square have solid reputations, with robust security measures. They're also easy to integrate into most website platforms. Remember, the ease at which customers can complete their payment process can significantly influence whether they proceed with the purchase or abandon the cart. On your end, reliability is vital; hitches during the transaction process can mean lost sales. Lastly, consider the cost. Many payment gateways charge fees per transaction, so factor these into your pricing.

Importantly, make sure that the payment gateway you choose is compatible with your sales funnel strategy. The gateway can help you keep track of customers' purchases, giving you at-a-glance data that you can use to refine your marketing strategies. It's also a good idea to consider a gateway that offers mobile compatibility, as a significant percentage of people now make purchases on their mobile devices. In a nutshell, a well-chosen payment gateway keeps your business running smoothly, inspires customer trust, and offers valuable insights to help grow your business.

Chapter 7: Optimizing Your Marketing Funnel

N ow that you've built an alluring web presence, defined your target market and crafted an engaging marketing funnel, it's time to hone and improve. Ensuring that you're squeezing every ounce of potential from your marketing funnel, this chapter will be focused on optimization. To start with, we'll delve into data analysis and review — learning to examine the cold, hard facts of your marketing performance objectively is fundamental in this digital age. We'll move swiftly into discussing A/B testing which can help you ascertain the best approaches and fine tune your funnel according to tangible consumer responses. Finally, we'll draw the curtain on Conversion Rate Optimization (CRO), elucidating how to increase the number of prospects who become customers even when traffic remains the same. By learning to optimize, you'll create a continually improving system that keeps your business moving forward.

Data Analysis and Review

After implementing your marketing funnel, it's essential to embark on the crucial task of analyzing and evaluating the data from your activities. These metrics will provide an insight into the areas where your funnel is performing well and where there may be room for improvement. Data analysis and review is the unsung hero that can transform your marketing approach.

Start with a careful review of your website traffic. This data will tell you volumes about where your visitors are coming from, which pages they're spending the most time on, what's drawing them in, and more importantly, what's making them leave. This key data can be easily tracked using tools like Google Analytics, which can offer you a often surprising glimpse into your website's operations.

After a thorough look into website traffic, go deeper by analyzing the behavior of your visitors once they're on your site. This includes aspects such as pages viewed, time spent on each page, clicks made, and more. Collecting and scrutinizing this data will give you a better understanding of how visitors interact with your website.

Don't neglect studying the demographics of your visitors as this can reveal who your typical customer may be. Analyze elements such as location, age, and even interests, if the data is available. This type of demographic data can assist in refining your targeting strategies to engage with the most relevant audience segments.

Next in line for analysis is your conversion rate, the percentage of website visitors who take the desired action, such as subscribing to a newsletter, filling a form, or making a purchase. The conversion rate is directly linked to the effectiveness of your funnel, and any anomalies present a valuable opportunity to fine-tune elements to heighten efficiency.

The bounce rate - the percentage of visitors who leave after viewing only one page - is another significant metric to consider. A high bounce rate can be a sign that pages are not compelling enough or don't match the expectations set by your marketing campaign. In-depth examination of your bounce rate can uncover whether your site's user experience needs improvement or if your content requires a revamp.

Importantly, keep tabs on your email marketing metrics too. You'll want to track your open rates, click-through rates, conversion rates, and unsubscribe rates. These can collectively give you a nuanced understanding of how well your email strategy is faring in engagement and sales generation.

Pay special attention to your lead magnets' performance. This can be easily done by tracking the number of people who interact with them, the number of leads generated, and ultimately, how many of these leads convert into paying customers.

Social media analytics should also be part of your review to measure the success of your social media marketing. Key measurements include reach, impressions, engagement, follower growth, and click-throughs. Monitoring these regularly will reveal which content strikes a chord with your audience and which platforms bring the most traffic and conversions.

A careful study should also be made of your sales page metrics. Knowing how many visitors arrive on those pages, how long they stay, and what percentage makes a purchase can reveal much about the effectiveness of your sales pitch and the overall user experience.

The insights gained from this data analysis can be turned into actionable steps for adjustments. It's all about refining and optimizing at every level of your marketing funnel. The ultimate aim is to create a seamless customer journey that transforms a casual website visitor into a loyal customer.

After interpreting all data collected and knowing where the opportunities for improvement lie, it's time to start planning for modifications. Changes that address the issues or gaps uncovered in your data analysis can significantly improve the performance of your funnel.

Remember, the data analysis and review process is not a one-time exercise. Keep in mind that it's an ongoing process, continually offering ways to improve and to keep your funnel performing at its best. Regular monitoring and immediate adjustments are the keys that can unlock long-term success for your online marketing campaign.

Also, in no way would you want to jump to conclusions without sufficient data. The more data you have, the more confident you can be about your findings and the decisions you make based upon them. So, give your marketing funnel the time it needs for enough data to be collected and analyzed, ensuring your interpretations and alterations are made from a position of strength.

Wrapping it up, the real power of data analysis and review lies in the insights it offers for continuous improvement. By paying close attention to your website's data, you can make informed decisions that will ultimately enhance your marketing efforts and drive business growth.

HOW TO A/B TEST YOUR FUNNEL

As we review the strides taken in building and implementing your marketing funnel, it's important to highlight that optimization is a continuous process. One important method to optimize your funnel is A/B testing. A/B testing is a powerful tool that can help you make data-driven decisions about your funnel, fine-tune your marketing efforts and improve overall conversion.

You might be asking, "What is A/B testing?" Simply put, it is a method used to compare two versions of a webpage or other user experience to determine which one performs better. It's a way to test changes to your webpage against the current design and determine which one produces better results.

To perform an A/B test, you will need to split your audience into two groups: one group sees version A (the 'control'), and the other group sees version B (the 'variant'). The performance of both versions will indicate which change is more effective and beneficial for your funnel.

However, setting up an A/B test requires strategy and careful thought. Your first task is to decide on your testing priorities. For instance, you may choose to test elements such as headlines, color schemes, calls to action, or media like images and videos. Keep in mind, the element you choose to test should have a significant impact on user behavior or experience.

Once you've picked an element to test, you'll need to choose your success metric or the goal you want to achieve. This could be increasing email sign-ups, boosting click-through rates, or raising conversion rates. It's crucial to set clear, specific goals to determine if your A/B test was successful.

With your testing priority and success metric set, you can now move onto building your A and B versions. Remember that version A is typically your existing design or 'control,' while version B hosts the changes you wish to test. Keep in mind that testing one thing at a time can help you accurately determine what's causing a shift in user behavior. If you test too many elements at once, you may not figure out what really worked or didn't.

Upon creating the variations, you'll need to split your website traffic evenly between them. This can typically be achieved using an A/B testing software which automatically allocates traffic to the different variations.

Following this, it's time to collect and analyze your data. Allow your test to run for a sufficient amount of time to ensure data accuracy. Rushing a test can lead to inaccurate results. Once the data is collected, analyze the results to see which version of your webpage performed the best.

If version B performed better, that's fantastic! You can now implement the changes on a larger scale. If version A remains the winner, that's still excellent news! You have gained valuable insights, and you can develop new hypotheses to test. Always remember that in A/B testing, there is no failure - there are only results and learnings.

It's vital to repeat the A/B test process frequently. Consistently testing different elements of your website can lead to continuous improvement and optimization of your funnel. Understand that no website is ever truly 'complete.' There is always an element that can be tested, tweaked, and optimized.

Finally, remember the significance of documenting your results. Keep records of what you tested, the results, and any changes done based on those tests. This documentation serves as a valuable resource for future testing, decisions, and team members.

A/B testing can seem a little daunting, but once you get the hang of it, it's a game-changer. Testing, learning, and optimizing is what marketing is all about. Embrace A/B testing as an essential tool in your toolbox to refine your marketing funnel and ultimately increase conversions and sales. Let the data guide you to a more profitable and successful online business.

CONVERSION RATE OPTIMIZATION

One of the pivotal points in maximizing sales through your marketing funnel is honing in on Conversion Rate Optimization (CRO). At its core, CRO is a systematic process of increasing the percentage of website visitors who complete a desired action, whether that be filling out a form, becoming customers, or otherwise. In this section, we'll delve deeper into how you can optimize your website's conversion rate and make the most out of your marketing funnel.

The first step in this process is understanding your user's journey on your website. From the moment a visitor lands on your page to when they exit, every step of their interaction matters. This comprehension of their user journey allows for better designing experiences that usher them through the conversion process smoothly.

Another vital aspect of CRO is taking a hard, fast look at your website's usability. Can visitors find what they're looking for effortlessly? Is the navigation intuitive and the design appealing? A website that is easy to navigate and visually pleasing can drastically improve conversion rates.

To gauge usability, employ tools like heatmaps, session recordings, and analytic platforms that offer insights into how your visitors behave. Understanding what leads to bounces and what promotes engagement can assist in knowing the right areas to tweak for optimization.

Creating a simple and clear call-to-action (CTA) is another crucial practice in maximizing conversions. The CTA button or link should lead customers to take the desired action, be it purchasing a product, signing up for a newsletter, or downloading a lead magnet. Testing variations of your CTA, in terms of wording, color, size, and position, can also drive significant improvements in conversion rates.

High-quality content is another backbone in the optimization process. It not only boosts SEO rankings but also persuades visitors to convert. Strive to deliver valuable, engaging, and easy-to-digest content that establishes trust and convinces the visitor to take the desired action.

Keep your website forms concise and simple. The less work visitors have to do, the more likely they'll complete the action. Reducing the number of fields, providing clear, concise instructions, and reassuring privacy can increase form completion rates.

Testimonials and reviews are powerful tools that build trust and remove doubts. Showcasing real-life examples of satisfied customers can influence potential customers to take the plunge. Try to incorporate these testimonials throughout the website, especially on sales or pricing pages, to boost credibility.

In line with your marketing funnel, make sure the solutions you sell align well with the problems your audience faces. Showcase how your products or services can solve their problems or meet their needs, to propel them towards conversion.

Crucial to the concept of conversion rate optimization is the idea of continuous testing and improvement. A/B testing, split testing, and multivariate testing are different methods you can employ to observe what works best for your audience. Making data-driven changes to your website and marketing funnel will ensure improvements in your conversion rate.

In essence, every element of your marketing funnel needs to work cohesively to drive conversions higher. A data-driven approach, coupled with an understanding of your audience's needs and user experience, can simplify and magnify the impact of your conversion rate optimization efforts.

This isn't a once-and-done process. Effective CRO requires a sustained effort, consistent testing, and iterative changes based on user behavior, industry trends, and website performance data.

A solid grip on CRO also opens up the horizon of opportunities to better understand and appreciate audience preferences, thus fueling strategies for retention and advocacy. The end goal is a coherent, user-friendly experience that drives positive action, creating a win-win for both customer satisfaction and business growth.

Remember, conversion rate optimization is an investment, not an expense. The time, energy, and resources you put into this process can yield significant returns by transforming more visitors into loyal customers. Embrace the practice of CRO in your marketing funnel, and witness the ripples of improvement it can bring to your online business growth.

Chapter 8: Expanding Your Online Presence

N ow that we've worked to solidify your marketing funnel, it's time to cast the net a bit wider. You've done well so far, but in this digital age, going beyond your website to reach your audience can make a significant difference. Let's begin by exploring affiliate marketing. It's all about making strategic partnerships with individuals or businesses who will promote your goods or services. You reward your affiliates with commissions for sales or leads they generate - it's like having an expansion of your sales team. A close relative to affiliate marketing, social networking isn't just about updating your status. Think bigger. Use it to build relationships, engage with your audience, share content and promote your goods or services. Sites like Facebook, Twitter, Instagram, and LinkedIn offer a unique opportunity for you to increase your brand's visibility. Finally, consider investing in paid advertising. This isn't a 'go big or go home' scenario. You can start small. Search engines and social media platforms offer various options like pay-per-click (PPC) and sponsored posts that will boost your visibility. Remember: the main goal here is to meet your customers where they are and engage them on platforms they enjoy to help drive them through your marketing funnel. So let's dive in.

Affiliate Marketing

Let's dive into the world of affiliate marketing. Affiliate marketing is a potent tool in expanding your online presence and ensuring your product or service reaches a wide audience. So, what exactly is affiliate marketing? In simple terms, it's an online commission-based sales system.

You partner with publishers or influencers who can sell your products or services for you.

By becoming an affiliate, these campaign managers gather an audience interested in your offerings and persuade them to make a purchase. In return, they take a fraction of the sale as their commission. This creates a win-win scenario where your products get promoted and sold, without you directly handling the sales process.

Now, let's delve into how you, as a website owner, can utilize affiliate marketing to your advantage. The first step is identifying products or services on your website that you believe will be attractive to affiliates. These might be high margin items or products with broad appeal for which a vast market exists.

Next, you'd look for affiliates. Affiliates can be bloggers, influencers, other business owners, or anyone who has a sizeable online following they can market to. Reaching out to potential affiliates should entail crafting a persuasive proposition that outlines the benefits of promoting your product, the commission on offer, support you will provide, and how their audience will benefit.

You need to ensure your offers and payouts are competitive in the affiliate market. If they're too low, potential affiliates may pass on your offer and opt for more profitable opportunities. On the other hand, setting payouts too high can reduce your profit margins drastically. Striking a balance here is crucial for both attracting affiliates and maintaining profitability.

Upon onboarding affiliates, you would have to equip them with the necessary assets to promote your products effectively. This could include promotional materials like banners, videos, and pre-written posts, as well as tracking links to monitor click-throughs and conversions.

Tracking is essential in affiliate marketing. Over time, you'll be able to identify which affiliates are most effective and produce the most ROI for your business. This data will inform future campaigns, allow you to refine your affiliate program, and build beneficial long-term relationships with the most productive affiliates.

Communication also plays an important role in the realm of affiliate marketing. Make sure you have an open line of communication with your affiliates. Regularly update them on new products, promotions, and any changes in the commission structure. Also, encourage feedback from them as they can provide unique insights into market trends and customer behaviors.

Managing an affiliate program may be demanding, but luckily, you can automate most aspects of it. You can take advantage of affiliate marketing software that handles tracking, reporting, payouts, and communication with affiliates.

A well-executed affiliate marketing program can significantly broaden your reach and boost your sales. However, it's not a simple task to establish and manage. It calls for careful planning, continuous monitoring, and regular tweaking. But when done rightly, this strategy can expand your online presence, and potentially raise your returns exponentially.

Bear in mind, affiliate marketing is not a standalone strategy, but an integral part of your larger marketing funnel. It's an effective way to lead potential customers into the awareness stage of your funnel and then, with the help of your affiliates' marketing efforts, guide them towards making a purchase.

Finally, don't overlook the importance of building good relationships with your affiliates. They are an extension of your brand, and their advocacy can significantly impact your product's reputation in the market. So, treating them well, paying them promptly, and showcasing your appreciation for their efforts will go a long way.

In conclusion, affiliate marketing is a powerful tool for expanding your online presence and your marketing funnel. It's a cost-effective way to reach out to a larger audience without excepting the effort and costs of individual campaigns. Implementing it correctly will undoubtedly enhance your sales and revenue.

SOCIAL NETWORKING

The digital era has seen an explosion in demand for businesses to have an online presence. With the ever-growing reliance on social networking channels for everything from catching up with friends to catching the latest news, not being on social media could be detrimental for your online business. It's no longer a bonus, it's a necessity.

Why is it so vital? Simply put, it's where your target market lies. Social networks are like huge pools filled with potential visitors, leads, and customers. It's where the people are. And where people are, businesses need to be. By leveraging social platforms like Facebook, Twitter, LinkedIn, Instagram, and Pinterest, you can extend your reach, build your brand, and most importantly, increase leads into your marketing funnel.

It's important to understand that each social network is unique, catering to different demographics and hosting distinct types of content. One size certainly doesn't fit all. For instance, if your target market consists of professionals, LinkedIn might be your best bet. If, on the other hand, you're aiming at younger consumers or trendsetters, Instagram and Twitter might prove to be more fruitful.

Once you've decided on which social networks to use, it's time to create your profiles. It can't be stressed enough how crucial it is to have a well-crafted and complete social media profile across all selected channels. Make sure to integrate your branding with a recognizable profile picture, engaging cover images, and a consistent business description. It should be clear who you are and what you do.

But being present isn't enough, you need to be active. Regularly post relevant, valuable, and engaging content to gain followers and retain the existing ones. This shouldn't be just about pushing your products or services, but also about providing value and building connections with your audience. Share blog posts, industry news, tips, and any other resources your audience will find useful or entertaining.

Don't only speak - listen. Social networking is a two-way street and requires interaction. Respond to comments, answer questions, and engage with your followers on a personal level. The more you engage, the more others will be inclined to do the same, which improves your visibility and reach.

It's also advisable to use social media platforms for customer service. Customers often turn to social media to air their grievances or ask questions. By responding promptly and professionally, you're not just resolving a customer issue; you're demonstrating your dedication to providing exceptional customer service. And that can win you some serious points in the public eye.

As for lead generation, social media platforms offer numerous opportunities. For starters, you can share your website's content—blog posts, resources, landing pages—to entice followers to visit your website. Furthermore, you can run contests, giveaways, or promotions that require participants to submit their email addresses, thus becoming a part of your email list, and consequently, your marketing funnel.

Additionally, most social media platforms offer paid advertising options. This is exceptionally useful when you want to target a specific demographic or reach beyond your followers. The advertising capabilities on these platforms are incredibly sophisticated, allowing you to narrow down your audience by a wide range of criteria. More on this in the next section.

Just like with any other marketing activity, it's essential to measure and analyze your social media performance. This will help you understand what's working, what needs improvement, and where you should be investing more. Most social networks provide some level of analytics that allows you to track engagement, reach, clicks, and more.

Social networks, if used properly, can significantly expand your business's scope. With the right strategy, regular and engaging content, and genuine interaction with your audience, these platforms can provide a considerable boost to your online presence and could take your marketing funnel to new heights.

Keep in mind, however, not to spread yourself too thin across numerous platforms. It's always better to conquer one or two networks than to have a negligible presence on all. So, understand your business, your audience, and choose wisely. And here's the last golden rule: on social media, always be authentic, be human, and be social.

PAID ADVERTISING

As part of expanding your online presence, paid advertising is one of the powerhouses of digital marketing. Once you secure a robust website and set up your marketing funnel, you're ready to dive into new pools of potential customers. Let's discuss how paid advertising allows you to reach an expansive audience.

Keep in mind, while organic growth and SEO hold vital roles in online marketing, they can't always deliver the speed and scope of paid advertising. Let's demystify the world of paid advertising - PPC, social media ads, display advertising, and remarketing.

Start with PPC, also known as pay-per-click advertising. The process is simple: you create ads that appear in the search engine results and you pay a fee each time your ad is clicked. Google Ads is the preeminent PPC advertising system. Use it to generate ads that appear in Google's search results. The real benefit here is speed - while SEO is a long-term strategy, PPC can deliver immediate results.

Next, delve into social media ads. Platforms like Facebook, Instagram, LinkedIn, and Twitter offer their own advertising avenues. These platforms allow you to target a very specific audience based on demographic details, behaviors, interests, and more. If you've clearly defined your target market, social media advertising could be extremely beneficial.

Remember, just setting up a handful of ads and sitting back will not guarantee your success. Testing and more testing is recommended to identify what works best. Be prepared not just to launch but to adjust, refine, and sometimes overhaul your advertising strategy based on performance.

Let's turn our attention to display advertising. Ever noticed those banner ads while surfing the web? Those are display ads. Unlike PPC advertising that works on a text-based format, display ads are all about catching the audience's attention with visuals. Use them strategically to build brand awareness and attract users to your website.

Remarketing (or retargeting) is another savvy online advertising technique to retain audience attention. Have you ever visited a website or viewed a product only to later see ads for it elsewhere online? That's remarketing at play. Using such a strategy can allow your business to stay top of mind among potential customers, increasing the chances of converting interested users into customers.

Even with these techniques, paid advertising can be a daunting venture without understanding the metrics. Track indicators like click-through rates, conversion rates, cost per click, and return on ad spend to analyze the effectiveness of your ads. Understanding these metrics will allow you to make informed decisions and get the best bang for your buck.

However, before you dive into paid advertising, take time to consider your budget. The costs can accumulate quickly, especially when you're paying per click or per impression. Therefore, have a clear plan on how much you're willing to spend and be ready to evaluate your ROI consistently.

Regardless of the platform or type, consistency is paramount in paid advertising. Consistent messaging, visuals, and value propositions across your ads can help establish your brand in the audience's minds. From a single banner ad to a sophisticated remarketing plan, maintain a consistent brand voice and image to remain recognizable and reliable.

Also, paid advertising is not just about gaining new customers, but also about learning from them. Look at your ad campaign results to identify trends and patterns in user behavior. This information is not just useful for future ad campaigns, but can also feed into other areas of your marketing funnel and business strategy.

In conclusion, paid advertising, when used effectively, can dramatically boost your online presence, drive traffic, and convert potential customers into actual sales rapidly. Remember, it's not about spending more but rather about spending smart, optimizing, and providing consistent valuable content to your target audience.

Chapter 9: Overcoming Common Struggles

You've wielded your newfound knowledge of online business, established a compelling website, and honed a highly functional marketing funnel. You've even broadened your digital footprint, but you're now facing a few hurdles that seem insurmountable. Fret not, this chapter aims to arm you with proven solutions for common roadblocks that can blunt your progress. We'll explore effective strategies for tackling customer objections upfront – instead of sweeping them under the rug. Managing technical problems can be daunting but with clear preparations, you can maintain your operations without major hiccups. Staying on top of your industry's pulse and adapting to market trends may seem like an overwhelming task. But, with the right tools and methods, it gets easier to keep your finger on the pulse of current trends without losing sight of your business's core objectives. The road may be riddled with a plethora of potential difficulties, but remember - behind every challenge lies an opportunity. So let's grasp those opportunities and clear the path for an untrammeled journey to success.

Handling Customer Objections

At some stage in the sales funnel, every online business will encounter customer objections. These can occur due to a variety of reasons, such as pricing, product value, or a customer's hesitations. Overcoming objections and turning reluctance into agreement is a crucial part of a successful marketing funnel.

Managing customer objections provides an opportunity for you to do two things: first, to fully understand potential pitfalls your customer might be facing, and second, to stress the value and benefits of your product or service to change the customer's perspective.

One common customer objection is the issue of cost. Many customers might find your product or service too expensive. Addressing this does not necessarily mean reducing your prices; instead, it could mean demonstrating an increased value to justify the cost.

You need to persuade your customers that the benefits of your product or service go beyond the monetary value. Highlight a return on investment or a cost-reduction benefit over time. Use case studies or customer testimonials that can reinforce your claims, and clearly detail how your product or service delivers value for money.

Another typical customer objection refers to the usability and quality of the product. Customers may believe that your product is too complex for their needs or that another product out there performs better.

Here, the power of showcasing comes into play. Provide customers with product demos or free trials to demonstrate how easy and effective your product is. Make sure to also highlight unique selling propositions that set your product apart from competitors. Remember, potential customers should clearly understand why your product is the superior choice.

A particularly nuanced objection comes when customers simply say, "I need to think about it." In this case, the customer has not explicitly identified an issue, but there's clear hesitation. Addressing this objection might require a bit more detective work.

Empathy and open conversations are vital here. Encourage customers to share their thoughts, worries, or doubts, and reassure them of any concerns. Consider creating a frequently asked questions (FAQs) section on your website, covering common queries and worries, as this can significantly assist in overcoming this type of objection.

Another situation you might encounter is when customers lack trust or fear online transactions. They might be looking at your products or services but are hesitant to make the purchase due to online security worries.

Address this issue by highlighting the security measures you've implemented on your website. Display secure payment badges and certifications prominently on your sales pages and during checkout. Offering a money-back guarantee can also bolster customer trust, as this helps convey that you stand behind your product or service.

Sometimes, customers may feel like they can wait, making the timing objection a concern. While your product or service might offer value and be of high quality, customers might still hesitate, believing that it's not something they require immediately.

Combat this objection by creating a sense of urgency. Limited-time discounts, bonuses on immediate purchases, or highlighting the consequences of not using your product or service right away can encourage customers to act promptly.

Remember, your customers are not enemies to be defeated but are partners to be guided. Your objective should be to address their objections convincingly and honestly. Providing quick and thoughtful solutions will not only help you gain trust but will also structure a positive customer experience that can lead to better conversions and long-term relationships.

Finally, regularly refine your marketing funnel, taking into account the types of objections that you frequently face. Your approach should always be proactive, solving problems before they become objections. Applying insights from past objections and continually fine-tuning your customer journey can significantly improve your conversion rates.

Above all else, listen. Customer objections often provide valuable insights into areas where your products, services, or processes can improve. By seeing each objection as an opportunity, you'll strengthen your marketing funnel and supply an experience that meets and exceeds your customers' expectations.

Addressing Technical Issues

Upon addressing customer objections, one must be prepared to face an inevitable yet crucial aspect of online business management: technical issues. Regardless of how meticulously a website has been crafted or how flawlessly the initial marketing funnel was implemented, there will invariably be glitches and hiccups along the way. It's essential to approach these setbacks not as failures but as opportunities to learn, adapt, and improve.

The immediate instinct when encountering a technical issue might be frustration or despair. However, remember every problem is merely a situation awaiting a solution. The first step is to isolate the issue. Be it a bug in the website's code, a faulty link in a sales page, or something as complex as a crashed server – understanding the very nature of the problem is half the battle won.

Next, you have to trace the timeline. Try to ascertain when the problem cropped up. Was it immediately after a new feature was added? Or maybe it was a day after you had sent several thousand marketing emails? By retracing your steps, you can unearth crucial information that likely holds the key to resolving the issue.

Once you've identified the issue, don't hesitate to reach out to tech support professionals. We exist in an age of specialization where chances are high that there's somebody out there who's an expert at tackling the particular issue your website is facing. Whether it's your web hosting service's tech support or a freelance IT professional, take advantage of these resources.

Meanwhile, you can't let a technical issue become a bottleneck that hinders your online business. Acknowledging the temporary issue while it's being fixed is a excellent strategy. Depending on the severity and nature of the issue, a quick message to your website visitors or an email to your clients mentioning the problem and assuring them of a swift resolution can go a long way in maintaining their trust.

Preemptive action is a significant part of addressing technical issues. Having multiple backups of your website and frequently updating them ensures that you can easily restore it to a previous state when things go haywire. Also, taking advantage of cloud services can offer an additional layer of protection and recovery options.

Another powerful way to tackle technical issues before they become significant problems is monitoring. Implement tools that constantly monitor your website, alerting you immediately if they find any anomalies. This can circumvent a lot of problems that otherwise might have gone unnoticed until they escalated and began causing real damage.

Technical issues can stem from a website not kept up-to-date. Just as you would maintain your physical store, your website also requires regular maintenance. This includes updating your website's platform and plugins, ensuring that your website's design remains both visually appealing and user-friendly, and improving website load speed which greatly affects user experience and SEO ranking.

For a seamless checkout process, ensure the links and payment gateways are functioning correctly. Also, optimize your lead magnets and landing pages regularly to steer clear of setbacks that might disrupt your marketing funnel's flow.

Downtime periods for maintenance should be scheduled wisely. It would be best to aim for times when your traffic is typically low - this might mean off-peak hours, or even after announcing it ahead of time to your users so they are aware and planning accordingly.

Training matters as well. Many technical issues that seem overwhelming at first become manageable once you understand what's going wrong. Keep up to date with the basics of the technology your site runs on, and don't hesitate to roll up your sleeves and step into the problem-solving process with your technical support.

The bottom line is, technical issues are par for the course in managing an online business. The trick lies in not eliminating them altogether, but in being equipped to handle them swiftly, efficiently, and, if possible, preemptively.

Addressing technical issues might seem daunting, but remember that every challenge overcome makes your business more resilient. By facing these problems head-on and building on the solutions, you build a stronger, more reliable business that can withstand the digital environment's constantly evolving nature.

In the next section, we'll discuss another integral aspect of owning an online business: keeping up with market trends. Till then, embrace the challenges and stride confidently knowing that you're becoming better adept at navigating the digital business landscape each passing day.

Keeping Up with Market Trends

The ever-changing nature of online businesses is both a blessing and a curse. Markets fluctuate, customer preferences evolve, and new competitors emerge seemingly overnight. Keeping up with these swift market changes is one of the biggest challenges website owners face. However, staying abreast of market trends doesn't need to be overwhelming. Consider it an opportunity to adapt, thrive, and enhance your business model further.

First and foremost, understanding what a market trend is vital. Indeed, it's any noteworthy shift in your industry's behavior, customer's preferences, or technological advancements that can influence your online business. Understanding these trends can mean the difference between success and failure.

Staying updated with market trends requires consistent research and the willingness to pivot your strategies when necessary. To begin with, set up your news aggregator or follow relevant blogs, influencers, and industry publications. By creating a habit of daily briefings on industry news and innovation you can stay ahead of potential changes, giving you a strategic edge over competitors who don't utilize this technique.

Aside from broad industry news, trends specific to online businesses and e-commerce are also worth exploring. Watch out for shifts in digital marketing strategies, changes in search engine algorithms, or emerging social media platforms. Keeping an eye on digital trends enables you to update and optimize your marketing funnels accordingly.

But how should you react when you identify a new market trend? The key is to approach change thoughtfully and strategically. Constantly overhauling your strategies with every single market shift can do more harm than good. Instead, analyze the trend, make a plan, and implement changes gradually to test and monitor their effectiveness.

It's also crucial to keep tabs on your competition. Keep an eye on their websites, social media platforms, and marketing strategies for hints about their next moves. Don't mimic their strategy, but use it as a starting point to analyze what tactics might work for your business. If they introduce a new feature or tool, consider how it may apply to your website or how it may change the competitive landscape, and plan your future moves accordingly.

Engaging with your customers directly is another critical method of keeping up with market trends. After all, your customers are the best indicators of market shifts. Send out surveys, encourage reviews, or monitor social networks to get an accurate pulse on their needs and wants. Consider incorporating this feedback into your marketing funnel to better serve your target audience and increase conversions.

Staying ahead of market trends majorly involves investing in technological advancements which can streamline your operations and improve your user experience. For example, many businesses are leveraging AI and machine learning to improve personalization and customer service. By being an early adopter of these technologies, you can stand out in a crowded market.

Cultivating a corporate culture that embraces change is also paramount in maintaining a flexible and resilient business. Encourage your team to be trend hunters, ready to adapt based on new industry shifts. This openness to change and eagerness to innovate can prove invaluable when maintaining competitive advantage.

Remember that not all trends are worth following. Evaluate each new trend against your company's unique context and goals. The last thing you want is to blindly jump on a bandwagon that's not aligned with your overall business strategy. Your commitment to keeping up with market trends should enhance and not distract from your fundamental business operations.

It's also worth predicting future trends if possible. While this may seem like a risky move, making educated forecasts based on current data and industry knowledge allows you to adapt before a trend becomes mainstream. Being a trendsetter rather than a follower can benefit your online reputation and brand image.

Keeping up with market trends is undeniably a challenging maneuver. However, by staying informed, adaptable, and mindful in your strategies, you'll be poised to continually refine your marketing funnel, satisfy your customers, and stay ahead of the competition. The world of online business is dynamic and fluid, but with the right approach, you'll be prepared to navigate the waves of change with confidence.

In this dynamic and competitive world of digital entrepreneurship, it's not enough to just create a marketing funnel and wait for the sales to roll in. The most successful online businesses constantly innovate, adapt, and stay ahead of market trends. Remember, the only constant is change. Embrace this change, and turn it into your superpower.

Chapter 10: Case Studies

After navigating through the complexities of setting up and optimizing a marketing funnel, it's time we inspected some real-life examples for better understanding. In this chapter, we dive into various case studies demonstrating how different businesses utilized marketing funnels to maximize their sales effectively.

Case Study 1: Bob's Online Bookstore

Bob's Online Bookstore is an e-commerce website working exclusively with books. Bob identified his conversion goal as selling more books. He began by enhancing his website layout, made sure it was user-friendly, and infused compelling content related to books. His primary target was book lovers and students.

Bob attracted potential customers through social media promotions and by consistently posting engaging book reviews to create awareness. These activities led interested individuals to his website, marking the beginning of their journey through his marketing funnel.

He then encouraged visitors to subscribe to his newsletter, using a lead magnet, a free eBook. The 'Thank you' page for signing up doubled as a landing page introducing highlighted books.

Email automation was used to engage subscribers, sharing new arrivals, discounts, and personalized reading recommendations. Notably, many converted into customers, thus leading to increased sales.

CASE STUDY 2: GETFIT HEALTH COACHES

GetFit, a virtual wellness platform, aims to provide personalized training sessions. Their target was fitness enthusiasts or those seeking to improve health and wellness.

GetFit took the SEO approach, creating valuable health and fitness-related content. They implemented a blog on their website, crafting content around fitness trends, health tips, and exercises, all optimized for search engines. This sparked awareness and driven web traffic.

Visitors drawn to the page were encouraged to sign up for a free personalized fitness guide, serving as the landing page and lead magnet simultaneously.

They then utilized email campaigns that highlighted the benefits of their coaching services, shared client success stories, and offered the first training session free. This created a strong value proposition resulting in a high lead-to-customer conversion rate.

CASE STUDY 3: BELLA'S HANDMADE CHOCOLATES

Bella's Handmade Chocolates, a small business selling specialty chocolates, targeted gift buyers and chocolate lovers. Bella decided to use social media heavily, showcasing her products with visually appealing photos and videos on social channels.

She drummed up interest with seasonal offers and discounts leading potential customers to her website. Bella then established a sense of exclusivity with a rewards club, where customers could sign up in exchange for a free box of custom sampler chocolates that acted as a lead magnet.

Members received early access to new flavors and member-only deals via email campaigns. Bella also used retargeting for customers who left items in their cart without purchasing, resulting in a significant boost in conversion rates.

These case studies demonstrate how the fundamental pillars of an effective marketing funnel can be adapted and tweaked based on the nature of the business and the target market. The major takeaway here is; there isn't a one-size-fits-all strategy. Don't be afraid to experiment, analyze, and most importantly, keep customer behavior at the heart of your decisions to maximize your conversions.

Conclusion and Next Steps

In conclusion, you've embarked on an extensive journey to comprehend and generate a quintessential marketing funnel for your online business, adhering to a robust and methodical strategy. From understanding the basic tenets of e-commerce and the importance of an impactful website to defining your target market and devising attraction strategies, you've comprehensively explored the world of online marketing. You've learned how to turn visitors into leads and leads into customers, how to optimize your funnel and expand your online presence, and how to tackle common obstacles. Now, it's time to take a bold leap forward. The path to perpetuating your online success entails planning for growth, ensuring continuous improvement through data analysis and A/B testing, and staying consistently updated about new marketing trends. Keep exploring, testing, and finessing your techniques, and never stop learning. The world of online business is continuously expanding, and with the arsenal of knowledge you've gathered, you're well-equipped to reach new heights and maximize sales. The concluding pages contain some recommended tools and resources to further assist you in this exciting journey. Congratulations on your progress, and here's to your continuing success!

Planning for Future Growth

As you refine your marketing funnel and witness success, it's crucial to start considering the future growth of your website. Thriving in the online domain doesn't mean resting on laurels; you should constantly evolve and adapt, foreseeing future changes and tapping into unexplored opportunities.

Your website is a living entity in the digital realm. It must continually adapt, expand, and evolve to leverage new opportunities and continue engaging your target audience. Here lies the importance of implementing strategies for scalability and future growth right from the onset. However, this doesn't imply hasty changes; instead, steady and strategic growth over time.

One way to plan for future growth is to set clear and measurable goals. This gives you a road map to success and provides quantifiable markers that tell you when you've reached certain milestones. Your goals might include increasing organic traffic, reducing bounce rates, increasing conversion rates, or diversifying sources of traffic. Just ensure your goals are SMART – Specific, Measurable, Attainable, Relevant, and Time-based.

Creating a scalable website design is another significant aspect. As your traffic increases or as you add more products or services to your portfolio, you wouldn't want your website to collapse under the pressure. A scalable site is built to handle growth, meaning that it maintains performance and functionality as it accommodates more content and traffic.

Besides that, it's crucial to keep an eye on emerging trends and new technologies. The digital landscape evolves rapidly; what works today might be outdated tomorrow. Stay updated with advancements in your industry, consumer behavior, search engine algorithms, social media platforms, and tech innovations. This will help you adapt your strategies accordingly and ensure you're not left behind.

Let's also talk about diversifying your marketing strategies. Depending solely on a single type of marketing – be it content marketing, SEO, social media marketing, or email marketing – can lead to stagnation. By combining different strategies, you mitigate the risk associated with changes in algorithms or policies and access a larger, more diverse audience.

Furthermore, consider branching out into new markets. If your website is meeting success within a particular demographic or geographic location, consider whether it could be adaptable to different groups. Research potential markets and evaluate if your offerings could fulfill their needs, and what changes might be required for successful market penetration.

Investing in automation is another significant step towards future growth. Automation tools can streamline operations, increase efficiency, allow scalability, and provide valuable data for decision making. Whether it's automating email marketing or customer service, such investments can free up time for you to focus on strategic planning rather than repetitive tasks.

Your customer should always remain at the heart of your growth plan. Soliciting customer feedback will not only help you improve existing experiences but also gives insight into potential avenues for growth. Ask for their opinions, responses to new ideas, or what they feel is missing. Engaged customers often provide the most valuable insights for growth.

Another important point to remember in planning for future growth is budgeting. As you scale up your operations, you'll want to ensure you have the financial resources to cover the costs associated with that growth. This might involve larger marketing campaigns, hiring additional staff, purchasing new software, or upgrading your hardware infrastructure.

Lastly, be prepared for challenges. Growth often involves venturing into the unknown, which inherently carries risk. Problems will arise, irrespective of how meticulously you plan. Remember that every challenge is an opportunity for learning and refining your strategies. Be resilient and maintain a thorough problem-solving approach.

Remember, the key to successful future growth lies in careful planning, steady execution, and an ongoing commitment to learning and adaptation. It may not always be easy, but with the right mindset, strategies, and tools, your website can continue to grow and thrive.

By planning for the future, you're not only preparing your website for success but also instilling a culture of innovation and improvement. It becomes a staple in your online business approach, setting you up for long-term prosperity.

In conclusion, given the rapid evolution of the digital landscape, planning for future growth is no longer a luxury, but a necessity. By sustaining growth, adapting to changes, and continuously engaging your audience, your website becomes a resilient entity, capable of thriving in the ever-changing digital world.

ENSURING CONTINUOUS IMPROVEMENT

Without a doubt, building a successful marketing funnel is a significant achievement. However, a static approach can only take you so far. Ongoing improvement and adaptation are a must when it comes to digital marketing landscape. Remember that to ensure performance progression, you must be committed to non-stop optimization and attention to the shifts in the market, audience behavior, and new technology trends.

The idea of continual improvement focuses on making small, measured adjustments to your funnel based on analytics and feedback. It's not about making massive conceptual changes all at once; instead, it's about fine-tuning the cogs in your system regularly to make sure it keeps humming along smoothly.

Firstly, always remember that your website and marketing funnel are not set in stone. One of the greatest advantages of digital marketing is that it can be changed and improved iteratively. This means that you can, and should, continuously test, track results, learn, and adjust your strategies accordingly. This could mean changing your visual design, modifying your calls to action, tweaking headlines, updating your content, or improving your SEO practices.

Keep a close eye on your analytics and regularly revisit your initial assumptions about your target audience and market. As businesses expand and grow, so do their audiences. What worked for your users six months ago might not have the same effect today. You must make sure your website and marketing funnel continues to meet the shifting demands and preferences of your users.

Moreover, don't be scared of updates and redesigns. As your knowledge about your audience and market deepens, these insights can guide updates to your website and marketing funnel. Redesigns and updates should always be based on data, not merely stylistic changes. An aesthetic refresh might look nice, but if it doesn't perform better in terms of engagement or conversions, it's not worth the investment.

A/B testing is an essential tool in your continuous improvement arsenal. This form of comparative testing allows you to change one element at a time and see how it impacts user behavior. You can then measure which version performs better, use the winning version, then continue testing to improve it more. It's a straightforward but powerful way to keep refining your funnel's effectiveness.

Conducting surveys or getting direct feedback from your audience can also be an effective way to identify areas that need improvement. Customer insights can help uncover issues you might have overlooked or highlight new opportunities to engage your audience.

Moreover, consider working with a digital marketing professional or consultant. They can offer advice drawn from a wide range of experiences and best practices, helping you spot patterns and opportunities you might otherwise miss. If budget is a concern, there are many affordable digital marketing courses and online resources that can provide a wealth of knowledge.

Set aside time in your schedule for regular review of your statistics, user feedback, and latest marketing insights. Staying abreast of these factors can help you spot issues or opportunities early and take action. Trying to cram this task in between other jobs leads to rushed decisions and missed details.

Lastly, embrace changes. Evolution is the key to long-term success in online business. Just because something worked well at one point, does not mean it always will. Be willing to adapt, test new strategies, and continue to develop your understanding of your audience and market.

Maintaining an attitude of 'continuous improvement' will not only keep your online business relevant and competitive; it'll also inject an element of exciting dynamism into your marketing, keeping you engaged, forward-thinking, and always ready for the next opportunity that comes your way.

In conclusion, ensuring continuous improvement is all about constantly evolving and adapting your website and marketing funnels to stay aligned with the ever-changing digital landscape. It's about focusing on what matters most - your users. If you keep them at the heart of your decisions, revising your strategies to meet their needs while considering the ever-evolving online world, you can't go wrong.

RECOMMENDED TOOLS AND RESOURCES

To thrive in digital marketing, there are several tools and resources that come highly recommended for creating, managing, and optimizing your marketing funnel. Following is a list of essential tools you might want to consider.

For starters, **WordPress** is a robust platform best suited for building websites. It offers exceptional scaling features, complete flexibility, and dozens of design templates. WordPress also provides plug-ins for further functionality, such as Yoast SEO for search engine optimization and WooCommerce for e-commerce capabilities.

While WordPress is great for broad feature sets, using a website builder like **Squarespace** or **Wix** can make things simpler if you're more design-focused. These platforms provide a seamless drag-and-drop interface and stunning visuals, while also simplifying SEO, responsiveness, and e-commerce setup.

When it comes to creating engaging and valuable content for your marketing funnel, **Canva** can be a game changer. It is a comprehensive design tool, allowing you to create visually impactful graphics for your website, social media, and email campaigns. Plus, there are plenty of templates to choose from.

In terms of managing and tracking user interactions, **Google Analytics** and **Hotjar** are necessary tools. Google Analytics captures broad statistical data while Hotjar offers user behavior analysis, heat maps, and more. These tools are key to understand your audience, what they're interested in, where they are having trouble, and which strategies are truly working.

For SEO, many marketers utilize **Semrush** or **Ahrefs**. These platforms allow you to understand the digital health of your website, discover backlink opportunities, conduct keyword research, and perform competitor analysis. They are indispensable assets for generating traffic and gaining visibility in search results.

For email marketing, platforms like **Mailchimp**, **SendinBlue** or **ActiveCampaign** come strongly recommended. These services provide easy-to-use email campaign builders, automation, segmentation, and tracking. Moreover, they help streamline your email marketing strategy, improving lead nurturing and conversions.

If you're focusing on social media marketing, then tools like **Hootsuite**, **Later**, and **Buffer** are staples. They allow you to schedule and manage posts across multiple platforms, track engagement trends, and offer insights into your social media success.

To build great landing pages that convert, tools like **Unbounce** and **Landingi** can be very beneficial. They focus on optimal design, copy, layout, and CTA button placement to help maximize your conversion rates.

For payment processing, consider **Stripe** or **PayPal**. These platforms offer secure, efficient online payment methods and integrate seamlessly with your website.

Additionally, they are trusted globally, which adds an extra level of confidence for your customers.

When it comes to A/B testing, tools such as **Optimizely** and **Visual Website Optimizer** (VWO) are often the go-to choices. They allow you to test website elements to determine what resonates best with your audience and leads to increased conversion rates.

Lastly, to harness the power of affiliate marketing, resources like **Commission Junction**, **Impact**, and **ShareASale** can be very beneficial. These networks connect marketers with relevant affiliates to help expand your brand's reach.

Keep in mind that while these tools and resources are recommended, it's critical to choose the ones that align well with your business needs, financial capabilities, and marketing goals. As you keep growing, your toolset may expand and change over time.

Investing in these tools and resources can give you a significant advantage in the market and ease the process of creating and managing a successful marketing funnel. With the right tools at your disposal, you're well on your way to maximizing the effectiveness of your marketing efforts.

In conclusion, technology is your ally in the realm of online marketing. Choosing the right tools will not only save you time and effort but also give you profound insights into your audience's behavior and needs. This knowledge is invaluable in crafting a marketing strategy that speaks to your audience and boosts your sales.

Appendix A: Glossary of Terms

E-commerce: This refers to the act of buying and selling goods or services using the internet, and the transfer of money and data to execute these transactions.

Marketing Funnel: A model that represents the customer's journey from the first point of contact with your brand (awareness) through the decision-making process, leading to a purchase (conversion).

Awareness Stage: The initial stage of the marketing funnel where potential clients become aware of your business and what you can offer them.

Consideration Stage: The stage in the marketing funnel where consumers are performing research, comparison shopping, and thinking over their options.

Conversion Stage: At this stage in the funnel, the potential customer has decided that they have a want or need and are going to fulfill it, most likely they are deciding who to buy from.

Affiliate Marketing: A form of marketing where a company pays third-party publishers to generate traffic or leads to the company's products and services. The third-party publishers are affiliates, and the commission fee incentivizes them to find ways to promote the company.

Search Engine Optimization (SEO): The process of improving a website's visibility in search engine results pages (SERPs), leading to increased organic (non-paid) web traffic.

Lead Magnet: This is an incentive that marketers offer to potential buyers in exchange for their contact information such as email address.

Target Market: This refers to a specific group of potential customers toward which a business has decided to aim its marketing efforts and merchandise.

Attraction Strategies: These are strategies used to attract potential customers to your website. They could include creating valuable content, social media marketing, and email marketing among others.

Email Automation: The process of sending out emails to subscribers, leads, and/or customers automatically, based on a schedule, or triggers that you define.

Landing Page: A standalone web page created specifically for marketing or advertising campaigns. It's where a visitor "lands" after they click on a link in an email, or ads from Google, Bing, YouTube, Facebook, Instagram, Twitter, or similar places on the web.

Sales Page: This is the page designed to convert visitors into sales or leads for a business. It persuades visitors to purchase or take up your offer by highlighting the best features and addressing potential objections.

Payment Gateway: These are merchant services provided by an e-commerce application service provider that authorizes credit card or direct payments processing for e-business online retailers and others.

A/B Testing: Also known as split-testing; it is the process of comparing two different versions of a web page or other marketing asset with the goal of determining which performs better.

Conversion Rate Optimization (CRO): The systematic process of increasing the percentage of website visitors who complete a desired action, such as filling out a form or making a purchase.

www.ingramcontent.com/pod-product-compliance
Lightning Source LLC
Chambersburg PA
CBHW051209050326
40689CB00008B/1247